"THREE (AND A SHIS

and other spicy tales from a sports writer's notebook

by RICHARD BOTT

Former Sunday Express chief soccer writer

FOREWORD by ALEX FERGUSON CBE

Front cover caricature by RAY ALLEN

Manchester
EMPIRE PUBLICATIONS

First published in 1998

EMPIRE PUBLICATIONS LTD
62 Charles Street, Manchester M1 7DF

© Richard Bott 1998

ISBN   1-901-746-02-X

Set in 11 on 13 point Calisto MT by
Michael Hubbard
and printed in Great Britain
by MFP Design & Print
Longford Trading Estate
Thomas Street
Stretford
Manchester M32 0JT

ABOUT THE AUTHOR

Forty years in full-time sports journalism. Thirty years with the *Sunday Express*, eight as a contributing freelance, 22 on the staff, as Chief Northern Sports Writer and then as the paper's Chief Soccer Writer. Author of 14 books. Has also worked in radio, television and PR. Now a freelance sports writer covering soccer and rugby league for the *Daily Mail*—the national newspaper he first joined as a sports sub-editor in 1964— *The Mail on Sunday*, *Ireland on Sunday* and contributing to numerous other sporting publications.

A full member of the Football Writers Association, of which he is northern chairman, and former chairman of the Speedway Writers and Photographers Association. Also a member of the Cricket Writers Club and an associate member of the Veteran Speedway Riders Association.

CHAPTERS

ACKNOWLEDGEMENTS

The title of this book was inspired by Barry Diamond, a footballing journeyman, who related one of his many funny experiences to the author over a pint in Topham's Tavern. The author's thanks are also due to carricaturist Ray Allen, for the front cover sketch, to Andy Searle at Empire Publications, for having the faith to publish and be damned, to Norman Wynne, for discovering that the "Empire" still exists, to a number of press colleagues and sporting celebrities, who have supplied anecdotes, and in particular to Alex Ferguson CBE, of Manchester United, the outstanding club manager of his generation, for kindly providing the foreword. Other publications which have provided sources of information and amusement include the excellent Umbro Book of Football Quotations, by Peter Ball and Phil Shaw and Colemanballs 6.

THIS book is dedicated to the memory of my first wife Maureen and to my second wife Sue, daughters Dany, Rowena, Kirstie and Laura and son Julian, another long-suffering Manchester City fan.

FOREWORD
by ALEX
FERGUSON CBE

MY relationship with the press has always blown hot and cold and it is a sad state of affairs that these days so many newspapers go down the road of sensation-alism and some sports writers seem prepared to sacrifice their integrity and reputations to keep their jobs.

The terrible problem for the tabloids is having to compete with the 'instant news' available on television from all round the world, on channels like Sky News and CNN, so the writers are constantly under pressure from their editors to come up with something sensational.

It might be about a player wanting to get away or a manager not getting on with a player. You seldom get managers betraying the trust of players in print but plenty of stories about players saying life has been hell under such and such a manager. And not just in football. Other sports, too.

What makes me really angry is when I am misquoted or quoted when I have said something 'off the record'. The writer is not always the one to blame but how often do you get a response if you call the editor? So the writer is the 'Patsy' who gets it in the neck, gets banned or told 'you'll get nothing more from me'.

If it's not his fault and he moves to another newspaper or his editor moves, things get back to normal but for how long? Trust is becoming a thing of the past. When I was a player and we went on European trips it was an adventure and the press lads would go with us to a club or a bar after the game and there was never a thought that they might be observing your behaviour and planning to write about it. That mutual trust has gone and I'm not sure it will ever come back.

There are still some very good writers about. People like Hugh McIlvanny, Bob Cass, Henry Winter, Patrick Barclay, Glen Moore and David Lacey. Columnists like Patrick Collins and Ian Wooldridge write some marvellous stuff. Then there are guys I work with on a day-to-day basis, like David Walker and Peter Fitton, good honest guys who take great pride in what they write.

Wee John Bean, who took early retirement at the Daily Express on health grounds, was never a problem and what a character! I remember laughing at his party piece, a one-footed soft-shoe shuffle, on my first trip into Europe with United and the Manchester press boys. Remember, it is not just about how you behave as a journalist but also as a person if you are going to create trust in a relationship.

Richard Bott is one of the 'old school' who I have known since I came to Manchester United. He is still involved but not so much in the 'rat race' and not so dependent on the whims and demands of editors. He has served his time and been fortunate to enjoy the good days in sports writing and the personal contact and relationship with managers and players that comes through in this book.

It is a good read because it is a true read and they are always the best. Some of the stories are so funny and humorous. It is a light-hearted look at sport and sports writing and obviously a lot of it is about Richard's own experiences reporting on football.

Sometimes, as a manager and because of the pressures and the intensity of the job, you forget the funny side. When you are committed and absorbed you are vulnerable to stories against yourself which only become funny in the cold light of day. Very often one of my players or Brian Kidd, my assistant, will say 'Do you remember that time you said something or other, it was so funny' and you can't recall saying it or you think you couldn't possibly have said it.

Ninety per cent of it is said in all seriousness in the intensity of the moment and it is only when you look back that you see the funny side. If only people would give managers the respect that their work deserved, they would be able to enjoy the funny side a bit more.

There are so many good stories about the real characters in the game and we have a lot of fun at our League Managers' dinner every year when we get a chance to relax.

This book is full of good stories and experiences about characters past and present, tales about football managers, players and fans and other sporting people as well as the funny side of sports reporting. I have enjoyed reading it because it is true life, what really happens in the game, and when you are in such a serious and competitive business, you need a good laugh.

Alex Ferguson

One

HOME TRUTHS, HALF TRUTHS AND NOTHING LIKE THE TRUTH

IT'S a funny thing but I don't seem to have had a circulation problem since I left the *Sunday Express!* Very few headaches, either. And that little wound between the shoulder blades has healed up nicely.

You may find this hard to believe, when I work in a business that flies more kites than Douglas Bader ever did, but I'm not much good at writing fiction. My only attempt at a novel foundered because the story-line was so thin it was positively anorexic, the characters were as wooden as the Horse of Troy and the typewriter—it was a long time ago—self-destructed out of terminal boredom.

So it seems logical, after 40 years in full-time sports writing, broadcasting, PR and one or two other peripheral activities, and with time to reflect, to toss a few memories in the air and tell a tale or two. They fall into three main categories (1) hand-on-heart true from personal experience, (2) mildly embellished, and (3) apocryphal. They are only the repeatable ones, of course. And whatever you do, don't take them or the occasional barb too seriously!

'THREE CURRIES AND A SHISH KEBAB?' A strange title, perhaps. And absolutely nothing to do with my eating habits. Perish the thought. When it comes to irritable bowel syndrome, mine is already in the Victor Meldrew class.

Three C's and a S K is, simply, the punch-line to one of the funniest TRUE stories I've ever heard about football and related to me in my 'local' by one Barry Diamond, a 'See-you-Jimmy' Scottish journeyman who played the game in the lower divisions and even lower with fire in his boots and a mischievous sense of humour.

In his own way, Barry was a diamond. Still is; a sort of northern, non-league 'Gazza', a bit of a hot-head who flirted briefly with the big-time and only really went up the ladder when he took up roofing. But I'm just jealous. He played for the Finnish club Oulun Palloseura in the European Cup in 1981 and on the winning side in a Wembley cup final—Colne Dynamoes 1 Emley 0, FA Vase 1988—and I'd kill for that. Anyway, it's a good tale, but I'll save it for later. A bit nearer to closing time!

You could say I'm getting a bit close to 'last orders' myself after forty-odd years in the 'spin' dryer but there is plenty left in the battery even if it's not the fun it was in newspapers. Not even sports writing, which used to be one of the best insignificant jobs in the world. By insignificant I mean that doctors and nurses and surgeons and fire-fighters make more worthwhile contributions in one day than sports writers do in a life-time.

Any delusions I had that the job was more than that were shattered in Fulham's press room a long time ago when the brown bowler hat on the bar established that Desmond Hackett of the *Daily Express*, one of my Fleet Street heroes, was present. And he was the one who was preaching the sermon. I believe he had a brother in medicine, who saved lives without trumpeting the fact from the back page of a daily paper with a multi-million circulation.

Now that television gives us wall-to-wall coverage, warts and all, live from around the globe 24 hours a day, newspapers are finding it harder to hold the attention of and hang on to their readers. Survival has become the name of the game, sensationalism too often the last resort. Circulation wars? The way some papers and writers are prostituting themselves, it's more like Circulation Whores! 'Want me to show you a good *Times*, duckie?'

So many of the decision-makers in newspapers these days, of either sex, are silver-tongued 'whiz kid' mercenaries who hop from one title to another like rabbits on heat. As someone said, so sweetly and perceptively, they have 'risen without trace'.

It is a good job the quality papers—like *The Times*, *The Guardian*, *The Mail* and *The Telegraph*—and their outstanding writers and columnists are surviving because somebody has to set the standards. 'Gutter Press' is not a pleasant term. Yet there are bad days when you almost despair of some papers aspiring to such heights!

Paradoxically, basic sports reporting, describing events and incidents, tends to be more accurate than in the pre-television era because it has to be. You can't say players from both sides were involved in 'a mass brawl' if the camera shows only two or three players were involved and it was 'handbags at five paces'.

The camera does lie occasionally. There was a time when it was popular for newspapers to add emphasis to a picture of a spectacular goal by running a line of dots from the scorer to the net. The *Sunday Express* showed a picture of an England-Scotland international which appeared to show a player leaping to head a glorious goal. So the picture desk ran a line of dots from the scorer's forehead to the top corner of the net and captioned the picture accordingly. Actually, the player had scored with a volley!

I have often said that sports editors are like nappies and should be changed regularly, for the same reasons. Mind you, I have tended to say it quietly. I've had 13 up to now, which may be quite apt!

That side of the profession has never appealed to me although I did dabble with it some thirty years ago on the *Yorkshire Evening Post* in Doncaster, when they wanted what they call a 'writing sports editor'. All it meant was I had a bit more say in what went in the paper and got invited to a few more boozy lunches.

Not that I have ever had the ambition or aptitude to be a top production man even before the technological revolution in the 80's. No more page make-up pads and 'hot metal'. Who says there's nothing new under the *Sun*? Now it's micro-chips with everything although I get the impression 'joined-up writing' is new technology to some.

I know a few old hacks who just can't fathom today's high-tech stuff. I saw one, who had made a spelling mistake in his story on his computer screen, trying to correct it with Tipp-Ex.

Generally, I prefer to be 'on the road' rather than permanently stuck behind a screen (it used to be a typewriter) in an office. Get out and meet the people. Be at the sharp end. That's where the real fun is. You can't beat getting a good bollocking from Alex Ferguson after someone back in the office has put a 'spin' on your last piece on Manchester United. Or being pinned against the wall of the dressing-room corridor by an angry player screaming 'You got me dropped, you bastard!'

Live by the sword, die by the sword. It's a fair maxim. Far more accomplished and distinguished sports writers than I have had to answer for an outrageous headline or their 'fair cop, I wrote it' character assassinations and vitriolic candour. Sometimes in a court of law. Certain columnists I know thrive on confrontation, others just snipe away merrily from the safety of their glass houses.

One such columnist, on a provincial evening newspaper, used to love having a pop at some of the biggest names in sport, safe in the knowledge that many of them would never read his barbs. Imagine his shock when he opened his post one morning and received a solicitor's letter on behalf of a victim, working abroad, who had been sent a cutting of the offending article.

No self-respecting journalist can go through his career without upsetting somebody. The job is intrusive and often opinionated, by definition. Nosy parkers with notebooks or tape recorders. That's as maybe. Good investigative journalism, in news or sport, is admirable. There are some doors that need to be kicked open, some stones that must not remain unturned and if the truth hurts, tough.

It has become fashionable to blame media pressure for anything and everything from the fall of the Government to a Test match defeat, from a royal divorce to a footballer's drink problem or a manager's sacking. 'We are La Stampa, no one likes us,' we sang during the soccer World Cup Finals in Italy in 1990, when a typical rift developed between the England squad and the media. But many a story summarily dismissed as 'total rubbish' one day has been substantiated another.

One of the reasons why there is so much friction between sporting celebrities and the sporting media, in the modern era, is the constant demand for sensationalism.

There was a time when digging the dirt and invasion of privacy was left to the 'rotters'—rhinoceros-skinned news reporters who would mug their grandmothers for a page lead—and their chums the paparazzi. And what a good name they've got after the tragic and violent death of Diana, Princess of Wales.

Sports reporters and columnists used to be allowed to write about SPORT and the very thought of becoming foot-in-the-door merchants was inclined to bring on severe attacks of gout. Now it goes with the territory. 'Hatchet jobs' and 'the real story' have become part of the back-bench vocabulary in 'Fleet Street'.

Not out of choice, I can tell you. But everybody wants to get into the ring, so to speak. If it's a 'poor news day', someone back at the ranch will take the decision to put a spin on an old story or harden it up. Who cares as long as it sells the paper or keeps the TV ratings high.

One former national paper sports editor was known to have rung round his regional soccer writers on a day when the diary was an empty page and instructed them thus: 'The splash will be "CRISIS" so come up with a story to fit it.'

I love the tale about the *Daily Star* golf writer who was covering the Ryder Cup in America when Bernhard Langer missed the 'simple' putt that would have retained the trophy for Great Britain and Europe. The writer telephoned his sports desk later to suggest the best angle on the story was 'Langer's heartache' because the quotes from Langer were 'brilliant but very emotional ... plenty of tears shed ... so don't go too hard on him. All the team are rallying round him.'

'No sweat, leave it to us,' he was assured. The next morning his paper splashed right across the back page 'NEVER TRUST A GERMAN'.

Then there was the *Daily Mirror* soccer writer who phoned his London desk to say there wasn't much doing in his area that day apart from the Aston Villa player Nigel Callaghan being a bit put out because his manager had recalled him from a loan spell at Watford when he wanted to stay. 'Great,' said the production man at the other end of the phone. 'Write it as an "I HATE VILLA" story.'

'But he didn't SAY that,' protested the reporter. 'No, but he will have done by the time you've written it!'

'Hardening up' is often the process of turning a 'could be' or 'maybe' story into 'will be' or even 'has', with the obvious effect on its impact. Then the splash sub can get busy. I know, to my cost.

I have also discovered the truth can hurt as much as the fiction. Touch a nerve or let the manager's secret out of the bag and you're in big trouble. Down the years I have managed to fall out with some of the greatest managers and coaches in football ... Sir Matt Busby, Joe Mercer, Malcolm Allison, Stan Cullis, Bill Shankly, Bob Paisley, Kenny Dalglish, Tommy Docherty, Jack Charlton, Alex Ferguson and many more.

Thankfully, I have never been sued or banned—although once I came mighty close to both with Liverpool over a story written in good faith but totally insensitive and distorted by the headline—or had a long-running feud with anyone. I still enjoy the acquaintance of most and the friendship of some. Hopefully, a little respect, too.

Football managers, in particular, have a tough job with a comparatively short shelf life. I have been based in the north west since 1964 and Manchester City, my adopted club, have had 21 managers in that time. Is there a serial killer loose at Maine Road? One of the jokes that grew out of a typical City crisis was about the fan who went on 'Mastermind' and said his specialist subject was 'Manchester City managers 1996 to 1996'. He failed because he could only name four of them!

I wonder how many football-mad kids grow up wanting to be managers. Not one, I suspect. Every kid wants to PLAY. Being a manager must be a bit like being a soccer writer. It's a substitute for playing, if you can't do it any more or you never had the opportunity or the talent in the first place.

Sports writing, whether it's soccer, cricket, rugby, golf, boxing, horse racing, whatever, isn't really work, if you are fan to start with. It is an extension of all your childhood fantasies and a fabulous privilege, particularly if the job takes you round the world at somebody else's expense.

Of course there are odd times when it can be a pain in the rump, the hassle, the waiting, the stress of meeting deadlines, 'dead' stories, confrontations with players, managers and sports editors, injury-time goals, extra time, missed putts, fifth sets, late finishes, goalless draws, delayed press conferences, obstructive stewards, extremes of weather, corridors or foyers choked with autograph hunters, limited access, queues to pick up press passes, flat batteries, cramped press boxes, broken telephones or calls that don't come through, airport check-in desks, long flights, traffic jams, lack of sleep, alarm calls, car breakdowns, train cancellations, hotel bars that close early, no receipts, unexplained expenses cuts etc etc.

That is when the job is about as glamorous as a sportsman's or sportswoman's life when they put in the blood and sweat of training and practice that people rarely see. Pumping iron, pounding the streets or the training pitch in the wind and rain, dawn starts in a deserted swimming pool, hour after hour in the nets, at the snooker table, on the practice green, on the river.

It's all a means to an end ... money. No, that's being cynical. I really meant the joy of winning or the anguish of losing, those very special moments in sport which the writer is privileged to share. What's a little extra suffering along the way, particularly if there are some good tales to tell?

The ones in this book are not intended to offend or embarrass class, colour or creed; simply to amuse. As Alex Ferguson writes, in his foreword, 'when you are in a serious and competitive business, you need a good laugh'.

Primarily, you need to be able to laugh at yourself. And here's one of my favourites.

The love-hate relationship between press and personalities is here to stay. As that larger than life character Brian Clough, master of the one-liner, said when Nottingham Forest were on tour and two of the travelling press corps appeared simultaneously from adjoining WC's 'That's the first time I've seen two s***- houses come out of two s***-houses!'

Two

IN THE PINK

SATURDAY night sports papers are a diminishing breed, sad to say. London gave up on them years ago and others around the country have gone by the wayside; their sales devoured, no doubt, by the remorseless advances of television and local radio.

Among the notable survivors are the *Manchester Evening News PINK*, the *Birmingham Sports Argus* and the *Newcastle Evening Chronicle*. In my youth, when most decent-sized towns and cities had two evening papers, the Saturday night sports editions used to hit the streets in all the colours under the sun, Pinks, Greens, Buffs, Blues, Whites, Yellows.

They were the magnet that drew me into a career in sports journalism. Don't ask me why. There was no comparable streak of madness in the family. It began in Glasgow, just after the Second World War, when I was at primary school and already obsessed with football and a Rangers team I never saw in the flesh but idolised via radio and the written word. Willie Waddle must have been my first footballing hero ... and me an Englishman!

I think Glasgow had two Saturday night sports editions and they fascinated me, even as an eight-year-old! The colour, the match reports, the action pictures. Then, when my family moved back to my native Surrey, a friend of my father's used to give me the *Portsmouth Evening News* GREEN when he had finished reading it. Portsmouth may have been in the next county but they were THE team of the time—First Division champions two years running, in 1949 and 1950. I remember that caricature of a sailor on the front page of the Green every week; two thumbs up if Pompey had won, one up and one down for a draw, both down if they had lost.

Jack Froggatt, one of Portsmouth's most versatile and brilliant performers—how many outside lefts can play centre half and vice versa for England?—was my new hero yet I never saw him play either. My Saturday afternoons were spent on the local recreation ground or watching the now defunct Guildford City in the Southern League or the reserves in the London League. But I lived for that Saturday night sports paper that painted such vivid pictures I could practically smell the grass at Fratton Park and hear the famous 'Pompey Chimes'. It was an all too brief romance.

In March 1949, just after Portsmouth inexplicably lost to unfancied Leicester City in the FA Cup semi finals, my father's job took him north again, to Yorkshire and the picturesque spa town of Harrogate; the place I still call 'home' because I spent most of my formative years there.

Right from the start, I was in my element, Saturday night sports papers-wise. Not one, but three. The *Yorkshire Evening Post* BUFF, *Yorkshire Evening News* GREEN 'UN and *Bradford Telegraph and Argus* PINK. Bye, bye, Pompey, hello Leeds United, Huddersfield Town, Bradford City and Bradford Park Avenue. My Saturday night reading now encompassed a strange game called Rugby League and the deeds of men like Lewis Jones, Ernest Ward and Geoff Gunney.

While some kids wrote off to clubs for autographs and badges, I wrote to evening newspapers around the country for their Saturday night sports editions and built up quite a collection. Much later I consummated my peculiar love for pinks and greens etc by writing for some of them, notably the three evening papers who employed me full-time, the *Coventry Evening Telegraph*, the *Birmingham Evening Despatch*— incorporating the *Sports Argus*—and the *Yorkshire Evening Post*. I also contributed regularly to the *Manchester Evening News* for eight years.

To this day, I am an avid reader of these coloured sports editions which are put together so professionally in such haste and find their way onto the streets within an hour of the final whistle. 'Running reports', half-time intros, cliche-ridden round-ups, corny and repetitive banner headlines like 'Capital triumph', 'Blue Murder' and 'Reds go nap' and infuriatingly incomplete results in the back page 'Stop Press' column, like 'Carlisle 2' are all part of the fun.

Sometimes great minds don't think alike. In the era when the Cha-Cha-Cha was enjoying immense popularity in the dance halls and night clubs, Bobby Charlton smashed a hat-trick for Manchester United. The splash sub on the PINK had a flash of inspiration and wrote an alliterative front-page banner headline 'CHA- CHA-CHARLTON'.

Unfortunately, in that particular type size it was one letter too 'strong' and, in the parlance of the trade, 'bounced'. The harassed stone sub, with only minutes to amend the headline before the page was due off, missed the point entirely and changed it to 'CHA-CHA-BOBBY'.

United have friends in high places. I'm not suggesting the *Manchester Evening News* is ever guilty of bias towards the boys from Old Trafford but when they suffered a rare tousing, someone in authority insisted the Pink headline be changed from 'Sad United in 6-1 drubbing' to 'Reds in 7-goal thriller'.

Literals abounded in the old days of linotype operators and 'hot metal'. What a difference one wrong letter can make. Examples: 'Roy Dwight was carried off with a broken log' ... 'Peter Osgood hit the bar with a shit from 25 yards' ... 'Charlie George shot wife after only ten minutes' ... and the classic about the player who 'pissed a fatness test just before the kick-off'.

If a linotype operator realised he had made a mistake he still had to complete the line of lead by tapping out any words or letters that came into his head. If he forgot to throw out the 'rogue' line and it got into the paper, as it often did in Pinks and Greens, it might read something like 'Jones shoft wideBOLLOCKSXXX'.

New technology has done away with the 'transposed line' when two lines of type went in the paper in the wrong sequence. I can quote you this example, from a Stoke City-Liverpool match report which appeared in the *Sunday Express*. The paragraph should have read: 'After a week of tribulation and humiliation, the Anfield answer was a battling 1-1 draw and goalkeeper Bruce Grobbelaar's response "We needed a good kick in the pants—now just watch us go".'

But because two lines were transposed, it actually read: 'After a week of tribulation and humiliation, the Anfield answer was a battling 1-1 draw and goalkeeper Bruce needed a good kick in the Grobbelaar's response "We pants—now just watch us go".'

Of course I WANTED to be a professional footballer above all else, kicked a ball from dawn until dusk and twice scored four goals in a game for Harrogate Town. The professionals say, contemptuously, you can't be taken seriously as a football writer if you haven't played the game. I've played it alright ... in back streets, back yards, gardens, parks, beaches, living rooms, scout halls, gymnasiums, recreation grounds, tips, tennis courts, bowling greens, alleyways, garages, school yards, small pitches, big pitches, gravel pitches, tarmac pitches, all-weather surfaces, indoors, outdoors, upstairs, downstairs, icebound, mudbound, fogbound, snow-covered, cobbled, wind-blown, rain-lashed, hail, sleet, thunder and lightning, floodlit, gas-lit, pitch-black, level, sloping, cow-clapped, short grass, long grass, no grass, in spring, summer, autumn and winter. And with every shape and size of ball that was ever invented, not to mention a few that weren't.

I have wept buckets after seeing my first real leather football, size 4 and a birthday present, roll under the front wheel of a double decker bus after chasing it nearly a hundred yards down a country lane from the local rec in Guildford's Onslow village. I can still picture the limp remnants lying in a congealed mixture of dubbin and French chalk. Is that where they got the expression 'dead ball'? The bus driver should have been shot at dawn.

People who have NEVER played a violin or a piano still appreciate good music, recognise quality and flinch at the jarring sound of a bum note. In football, I got as far as the West Yorkshire League with Harrogate Town and lacked the ability/bottle/balance/vision/synchronization/pace/speed of thought/co-ordination/dedication (perm any number) to go any further. But DON'T try telling me I never played the game!

Cricket, likewise, although never with quite the same passion. At one stage of my amateur sporting 'career', I scored more goals than runs, which was a bit embarrassing since I was an opening batsman! I believe I may hold some sort of record in the 'first-ball duck' stakes.

I was opening the batting for R. Ackrill Ltd—my first employers and publishers of the *Harrogate Advertiser* and various other weekly newspapers in what is now known as North Yorkshire. It was a 20-overs-a-side game on a balmy summer's evening at Summerbridge in Nidderdale and I took rather a good catch, sprinting round the long-on boundary to pluck the ball one-handed out of the sky.

But when we began the chase for the 78 runs we needed to win, I was out first ball, lbw, bowled and caught behind. Take your pick. In sheer terror I played back to a quickish delivery from a farmer built like one of his own outhouses and the ball nicked the pad, round about knee high, then the inside edge of my defensive bat, removed the bails and was gloved by the wicket-keeper standing back.

The umpire, one of our own lower order, as is the way in 'coarse cricket', looked suitably bewildered and didn't know whether to raise his index finger or all ten. I believe there is a tie for members of the 'First Ball Club'. I should have been entitled to a two-piece suit, a shirt and a pair of shoes after that humiliation. Did we win the game? Who bloody cares?

I did have my moments, with bat and ball, and at various other sports and pastimes; before and after I went into journalism. But the desire to be a sports writer was overwhelming and I put it down to my strange fascination for Saturday night Pinks and Greens, the sports pages of the *Daily Express*, Desmond Hackett and Henry Rose, supporting Leeds United during the emergence of the great John Charles and a magical experience that finally removed any lingering doubts or fears.

On a trip to London, in the early 1950's, to see a schoolboys' international at Wembley, I was 'drawn' like a moth to a flame to walk down Fleet Street on the Saturday night to pass the time before catching the midnight train back north. The place was alive. There was something about the noise, the smell, the vitality, the excitement, that was like Christmas and end-of-term rolled into one. I was hooked.

Whenever careers officers visited Harrogate Grammar School and asked what any of us wanted to be, the 'don't knows' were always in the majority. I never wavered. First hand up every time. 'Sports writer, sir.'

Wanting and getting can be poles apart. My parents wanted me to go into local government, banking or architecture. Safe job. Believe it or not there were such things in those days! They wanted me to stay on and spend two years in the sixth form. They would have got their way but for a brilliant stroke of luck. On the other hand, I came within a whisker of being expelled!

I had barely taken my 'O' levels when an advertisement appeared in the *Harrogate Advertiser* for a 'learner sports reporter'. It was manna from heaven. The stroke of luck was that I got the job a month before my exam results, which were so bad they wouldn't get me a paper round in this day and age.

The editor-in-chief of the Ackrill Group, one Robert H. Stockton, and I have to say a man of impeccable taste, seemed sufficiently impressed with a log I had kept of a scout trip to Norway and my opinions on Leeds United and John Charles. I was appointed on a six-months trial.

I cannot recall having seen a vacancy advertised in the previous twelve months and the post was not available again until I moved on some four and a half years later. So somebody was watching over me when that opportunity presented itself.

And I nearly blew it!

A few days before I was to be interviewed for the job, I skipped school to climb over the fence at the County Ground, St George's Road, to watch Yorkshire's annual match. They had a team of test cricketers in those days, in the mid-Fifties, Len Hutton, Frank Lowson, Willie Watson, Johnny Wardle and, of course, F. S. Trueman. But why did they only come to Harrogate for a midweek fixture and in term time, too? And why did half of the boys in the fifth year seem to have the same idea that particular afternoon?

Surely it didn't matter that much. The exams were over, even the teachers were winding down for the summer holidays and the temptation was just too great. Hutton and Lowson or Spanish and Maths? It was 'no contest'.

But the headmaster, Mr Carr, who actually lived in our road, was livid and more than a dozen of Class 5A3 were summoned to his study after morning assembly. Each excuse was more feeble than the last and the head's patience was wearing thinner than his bamboo cane. Mine was going to be that I had a bilious attack. At that moment, the door opened, an ashen-faced class-mate came out and I heard the head's voice thunder: 'The next boy who says he had a sick stomach is going to be expelled. I know you were all at the cricket.'

Panic gripped me like a vice because I was next in line. Suddenly, I remembered I had the letter from the editor of the *Harrogate Advertiser* in my blazer pocket. 'And what is your excuse, Bott?' demanded the headmaster. With a mixture of bravado and desperation, I pulled the envelope from my inside pocket and lied through my teeth: 'I had an interview for a job, sir ... on the *Advertiser* ... and I forgot to tell the form teacher ... I'm sorry, sir ... but I was so excited about it because it's what I've always wanted, sir.'

The head, who looked like Will Hay in his gown and mortar board, eyed me with a degree of suspicion. 'Did you get the job, then?' It was muck or nettles now, I was in too deep. 'I don't know, sir ... they are going to let me know.' All the head had to do was open the envelope and he would have seen I had lied, that the interview wasn't until the following week. I would have been out on my neck, humiliated and a million miles away from that job opportunity. Thankfully, he didn't. I was despatched with a flea in my ear that I wouldn't last ten minutes in ANY job if I didn't act more responsibly.

I often wonder what would have happened if I had 'come clean' about the cricket or stuck with my 'bilious attack' story. I know I will be eternally grateful that the head believed my little white lie ... even if Glamorgan did beat Yorkshire by four wickets!

Three

BIRTHS, DEATHS AND MARRIAGES

ON the basis that you can't expect to run a marathon until you get enough miles in your legs to give you half a chance of making the distance, the best place to start a career in newspapers is at the bottom.

A university degree is all very well (I wish I had one!) but those who use it as a fast track to the nationals don't know the string, never mind the ropes. A proper apprenticeship never did anyone any harm and it CAN be fun!

I joined the R. Ackrill Group of weekly newspapers in Harrogate on July 19 1955 and it was like winning the pools. But if ever a young lad was less suited to the rough old world of newspaper reporting, I would like to have met him. I was so timid it was six months before I was comfortable answering the telephone if anyone else was in the claustrophobic brush cupboard we called the sports department.

Street-wise and confident at 16? I was scared of the tea-pot. That nervousness manifested itself when, after my six months trial, I was switched from sport to news as part of my new three-year indentures. What did I know or care about anything except sport? Just when I was getting the feel of the business, I found myself under the wing of a short-tempered news editor whose crustiness owed much to the fact he had been stricken with polio and clearly envied the youth and athleticism of his ever-changing team of reporters.

I had an additional cross to bear. Lol Walker despised sport and sports reporters. On the first morning after my temporary transfer from the brush cupboard to the reporters' room, I was summoned to his office three floors below and told in no uncertain terms why the *Harrogate Advertiser* and its brothers and sisters was part of the fabric of Yorkshire life:

'Get this into your head, Bott. You will never get anywhere in this business writing about sport. Sport is for morons. It is a waste of space. And nor does news sell weekly newspapers. Only three things do that. Births, deaths and marriages.'

An hour or so later, after twiddling my thumbs and throwing paper darts at the lamp shade, I was summoned again—for my first news job. 'The gas board are digging up the road right outside the office. Find out why,' demanded the news editor. I must have spent half an hour trying to pluck up the courage to ask one of the gas board workers what was going on. One by one, they disappeared into a little canvas hut or the pub on the corner until only one remained. As he climbed out of the hole and straightened his cap, I blurted: 'Excuse me, I'm from the *Advertiser.* Do you mind telling me what you're doing?' He gave me a disdainful look and said: 'Yeh. I'm going for me bleeding dinner.' So ended my first news interview. And you think I'm kidding!

I spent six months on the news side, the first half of 1956. Round about the middle of February, Harrogate was hit by a particularly severe cold spell and, being a town 500 feet above sea level and inhabited by vast numbers of elderly residents, that was the signal for a boom in the undertaking business. It had never registered with me before, although I had lived in the town for seven years.

Suddenly, instead of covering the occasional funeral and writing it up in the house style 'The death occurred last Wednesday of the former Harrogate businessman etc, etc. The funeral took place at etc, etc. Family mourners were etc, etc. Other mourners included etc, etc, representing etc, etc,' we were doing as many as six a day. Normally, when one of the news reporters called at a funeral parlour or workshop, there was time for a cup of tea and a cigarette with the lads, maybe even a kickabout. Now they were knee deep in wood chippings and one was so knackered he slept in one of his own coffins.

The Advertiser dutifully covered every funeral, though some were considerably more important than others and the list of mourners often stretched well into three figures. Occasionally, two staff reporters were sent to the same funeral, standing by the door of the church or the crematorium collecting business cards. This particular winter, the number of funerals in the Harrogate area must have broken all records and it did become rather monotonous churning out obituary after obituary. The two long-serving sub editors were kept so busy they just tick-marked the copy and sent it down to the type-setters.

I am about to reveal a forty-year-old secret of some shameful black humour which I was only a party to in that I didn't bring it to the attention of the sub editors. Nor did any of the other news reporters until it became a monster and we put a stop to it ourselves.

He told us one of his favourite stunts, on a summer's day, was to walk through the Valley Gardens with a couple of his pals, and as they passed a park bench full of old folk sitting like cardboard cut-outs, say in a loud voice 'And do you know what she did next with the cucumber?' Then walk on 20 yards and look round at the shocked faces gawping at him with ear trumpets cocked. Definitely not a full shilling.

'I'm bored with all these funerals and lists of old farts representing this, that and the other,' he said. 'I bet the families have never heard of half the people who turn up, even the ones who seem to have season tickets! I'm going to liven things up. Add a few spicy names ... just to see if there is any reaction.'

Nobody believed him for one moment until Saturday's *Advertiser* came off the presses. There it was in black and white. He had added to the 'other mourners' at a particularly well-attended funeral, the names 'Mr W. Hipping' and 'Mr B. R. East'. The sub editors had not spotted anything untoward and it seemed a fairly harmless joke at first, if clearly in bad taste.

But as the lethal cocktail of ice and influenza claimed more victims, our weird colleague dreamed up more fictitious mourners with names that had sexual connotations, e.g. 'Mr and Mrs A. Ball-Breaker', 'Mr S. Trap', 'Mr C. Hains' and 'Mr F. Ewe'. They were slipped into long lists of mourners, individually, to avoid arousing suspicion. He stopped just short of using 'Mr F. Lagulation' but his prototype, 'Mr W. Hipping', became a 'regular' at almost every major funeral service for the next month.

Finally, outrage got the better of juvenile antics and we said 'enough is enough', though not until the obituaries one Saturday included what Kevin called his piece de resistance, the 'funeral' of 'Mr W. Hipping'. Written in the house style it went something like this: 'The death occurred on Monday in the Bahamas of the well-known former Harrogate businessman Mr W. Hipping. He died at his home in Nassau after a short illness, aged 78. Mr Hipping had lived abroad for some time although he did make frequent visits to his home town. A close friend and former business associate Mr B. R. East was among the small band of mourners at the funeral on Thursday.'

Incredibly, the newspaper received a letter the following week from an old lady who said how sorry she had been to hear of the death of Mr Hipping and asked us to convey her condolences to his family. She said she had never met the gentleman but understood he was a friend of her late husband because he had attended his funeral!

Before he disappeared into the mists in search of new bizarre adventures and escapades, Kevin could not resist a parting shot. It was an era when hula hoops were selling like hot cakes ... or even like hula hoops. (I must make a mental note to 'avoid cliches like the plague'). As the craze subsided, the news editor sent Kevin out to ask local toy traders what they felt would be next to catch the public's imagination. Perverse and perverted as ever, our resident crackpot concocted a story that 'whips and tops are set to replace hula hoops as the latest craze, claim Harrogate toy traders'. It was given a prominent single column on the main news page. I wish I'd kept the cutting.

The *Advertiser* was quite a staid, Victorian publication in those days, a broad sheet with adverts taking up the whole of the front page. The mid-week edition, the *Harrogate Herald*, and sister publications like the *Ripon Gazette, Knaresborough Post, Wetherby News* and *Thirsk, Bedale and Northallerton Times* were much livelier in presentation and content.

After six months of rotary club lectures, funerals, juvenile courts, council meetings, taking tea with centenarians who had somehow survived the flu blitz, hospital watch, police, fire and ambulance calls it was a blessing to return to the joys of local cricket and football. I did 'leave' news with a little more respect from the news editor.

One evening, when all the other news reporters had gone home and my last chore was to take a letter from the news editor round to the Town Hall, he summoned me in a panic. Standings, one of the town's oldest and most famous grocery stores and restaurants, was ablaze. 'You are the only one here until I can get hold of one of the senior reporters,' he bawled. 'So get up the street and see what you can find out.'

The scene was like something out of a movie. Flames leaping from the roof, firemen on ladders with hoses on full power, the street cordoned off and a large, ghoulish crowd of rubber-neckers.

I was so naive that I knew nothing about protocol, that unlike sport where doctors and dockers, window cleaners and sales executives were just cricketers or footballers, real life had rules when it came to who you questioned. There was a pecking order of spokesmen and women.

That never crossed my mind the day of the Standings fire. The store was owned by the chairman of the rugby club, one of the firemen up the ladder closest to the inferno was a local footballer and so was one of the policemen on duty. I nipped under a rope, went everywhere I shouldn't have including a tour of the gutted building as soon as the flames had been doused. I was accompanied by one of the chief fire officers, another local sporting celebrity, who seemed to admire my cheek.

I splashed my way across the flooded carpet of the first-floor restaurant, water still pouring from the bakehouse above—where the fire had started—and running like a waterfall over displays of cakes and chocolates. All good colour stuff for an eye-witness account. Quotes from the fireman up the ladder, from the store owner, the restaurant manager etc. Not bad for the office junior since the senior reporters who had arrived on the scene were kept behind the barriers until an official statement was released. My reward? A page lead and the mother and father of a rollocking from the news editor for breaking all the rules of protocol!

Tact was not one of my strong points. Once, when I was umpiring in a cricket match between Ackrills and a Nidderdale village team called Dacre Banks, I gave the managing director out lbw first ball. He had swaggered to the crease, immaculate in his spotless whites, new calf-skin pads, silk cravat and public school cap and taken guard, extravagantly, with his gleaming Gunn and Moore bat. But he was plum!

When I raised my finger, he froze for a few moments in utter disbelief, turned purple with rage and then stormed off muttering some dreadful obscenities. The fielding side watched him go, mesmerised. It was one of those still summer nights in the dales when the only sounds were of bat on ball, sheep baaing and the rumble of a tractor's engine somewhere in the distance. The managing director of Ackrills reached the visitors' dressing room and we half expected him to go through the closed door like 'Desperate Dan'. He disappeared inside. Seconds later, the sound of his bat crashing against the wall echoed around the valley. It was a demonstration of petulance and pique to rival any I can recall over the years.

'That your gaffer, lad?' queried the bowler at my elbow. 'Yes,' I replied. 'Don't fancy your chances much. Want to come and work on our pig farm?'

My only previous encounter with the MD had been less than exhilarating. In my first few weeks on the staff, I was a glorified tea-boy except that there was no kitchen, no canteen and no kettle. Also it was frowned upon to nip out to the nearest cafe. No doubt the editor and the MD made their own arrangements. There was a kettle and a gas ring in the photographic department two doors up the street. The trick was to get back into the main building, with the teapot, and negotiate the stairs to the third floor without being intercepted by anyone on the management floor.

I took to hiding the teapot inside a brown paper bag as I carried it upstairs—until the morning the MD appeared on the second-floor landing and demanded to know why I was carrying a paper bag with steam coming out of it. On that occasion, unlike in the headmaster's study, I told the whole truth and nothing but the truth and it was the sports editor, my immediate boss, who copped for an earful.

Stanley Wilkinson, 'Idle Stan' as we called him because he came from the Bradford suburb of Idle, was an excellent tutor and also a good friend who later joined the *Yorkshire Evening Post* in Doncaster and fixed me up with a job after my first experience of being made redundant. He liked his cricket, did Stan, almost as much as the Condor tobacco he stuffed in his pipe and polluted the 'brush cupboard'.

About the only time he didn't light up his quaint Sherlock Holmes pipe was when he opened the batting for Ackrills. I was the mediocre if willing protege he was determined to develop into an opening partner and seam bowler. At least the thought was there. And I was as fit as a butcher's dog from all my sporting activities. The trouble was, I batted like one.

My colleague in the sports department was Howard Walker, an eccentric who smoked 'camel dung' cigarettes and only had to take his jacket and tie off to be ready to play cricket because he always wore a white shirt and kept it buttoned at the neck and sleeves, always played in his black shoes and invariably put the pad on the wrong leg when he batted at No 11. He was, to be fair, also a walking encyclopaedia when it came to sport.

Weekly newspapers are wonderful breeding grounds for journalists. In my three and a half year apprenticeship, which embraced a six months trial and the NUJ (National Union of Journalists) Training Scheme, I was taught the basics of writing, reporting, interviewing, sub-editing, stone subbing, page make-up, headline writing, essential law for journalists, shorthand, proof reading and correcting ... and brewing tea. I was despatched at various times to our branch offices in Ripon, Thirsk and Wetherby and, when the company bought the *Pudsey News* and the *Horsforth News*, on 'foreign' trips to the other side of Leeds.

That was Len Hutton country. The famous Yorkshire and England opening batsman was the guest speaker at a cricket dinner I attended at Thorp Arch and used a fair bit of industrial language to embellish some of his anecdotes. He was well received and sat down with a self-satisfied grin. Imagine how his expression changed when the chairman called for a vote of thanks—from a local clergyman!

I reported on every sporting activity from polo to pigeon racing. Polo on The Stray at Harrogate, was part of the annual summer fete and gala one year. Marquees, pink champagne and plum-in-the-mouth accents. Then a cuckoo landed in the nest.

A working-class family from Halifax watched in total bewilderment as the gentry galloped up and down, all twills and sticks and snorting horses, and then headed for the nearest exit. 'Bollocks to this,' said the father, who looked as if he had landed on another planet. 'We're not staying here, Aggie. I thought polo were played in "watter" and there's no bloody pies anyway.'

Where, I wondered, did he expect to find the 'watter' in the middle of Harrogate's proud acres of green; although, come to think of it, the spa town is advertised as a holiday resort and people have been known to ask the distance to the pier or the beach. Seventy miles ... give or take a yard or two!

Good weekly papers, the *Herald* and the *Advertiser*. But even their conservative standards dropped as they abandoned long-standing traditions and sought greater impact. A good fifteen years after I left, my mother was so horrified by the banner headline on the main sports page of the *Advertiser* that she sent me a copy. Harrogate Town, my old football club, had been knocked out of the FA Vase by a controversial injury-time penalty. The headline, across six columns, read: 'VASE-CTOMY THE UNKINDEST CUT OF ALL'.

A final memory from my own days at Ackrills. It still makes me chuckle. The women's page had a paragraph tucked away in the cookery section. It read: 'Last week we printed a recipe for Banana Trifle. We apologise for any confusion or inconvenience caused by omitting bananas from the list of ingredients.' A mere trifle.

Four

HANG THE EXPENSE

EXPENSES. Now there's a subject close to every journalist's wallet. As a Fleet Street editor said sarcastically to one of his hacks 'If you used as much imagination in your writing as you do in filling out your expenses every week, you'd be an award winner.'

Filling or fiddling? There are a few Yehudi Menuhin's amongst us but hundreds of others are lucky to get the price of a corned beef sandwich. And many a 'gravy train' has been shunted into a siding or permanently removed from service as budgets have been tightened. The few shillings I was recompensed in my early years, even when I left Ackrills and joined the first of my three evening newspapers, the *Coventry Evening Telegraph*, were neither here nor there. You don't get paid mileage for riding to work on a bicycle. And the thought of 'entertaining' never even crossed my mind until much later when I discovered the Aladdin's Cave of goodies that reporters on the 'nationals' talked about over their large brandies.

What I love about expenses stories is the constant theme of trying to justify the most extravagant, outrageous claims and battles won and lost with heads of department and management do-gooders. I have collected a few expenses tales over the years which might just amuse you, if not the jackals of the Inland Revenue. Naturally, there is not a grain of truth in any of them!

There was the reporter on the *Liverpool Daily Post*, a newspaper not known to squander vast amounts of its resources on expenses, who was sent to cover the Isle of Man TT races and made the journey to Douglas by ferry. Soon afterwards he was asked to explain why, when he had been travelling alone, he had put in a claim for TWO breakfasts on the outward trip. Sharp as a tack, he replied: 'It was a very rough crossing and I brought the first one back!'

It is absolutely essential to have a convincing line ready for such inquisitions unless you are so highly regarded by your employers that : a) you can sign your own eccies; or b) you are beyond reproach.

Take the sports columnist on one of the tabloids who was taken to task over a fairly expensive lunch bill he had submitted. SPORTS EDITOR: 'You're not getting away with this one. It's obvious you took out the wife and kids because it's got two children's meals on it.' COLUMNIST: 'No, mate. That's two jockeys. They can only eat half portions!'

Or the rugby league writer who was challenged by his sports editor over a mileage 'discrepancy'. SPORTS EDITOR: 'How can you possibly justify putting down a round trip of 150 miles for going from Bradford to Keighley?' RUGBY LEAGUE WRITER: 'Roadworks and diversions!'

Some years ago, a nauseating management executive in the Manchester office of the *Sunday Express*, whose nick-name was 'Hissing Sid', tried out his 'frightener' tactics on me. He was wandering through the editorial department when I was doing my eccies. 'Hope you don't fiddle YOUR expenses, Richard ; it's a sackable offence.' 'Every week, without fail,' I replied, to his obvious astonishment. I elaborated. 'While you lot insist that the petrol chits for the company car match the mileage for the week PRECISELY, I'll carry on fiddling. And I suggest you must be doing the same.

'Nobody starts the week with a full tank of petrol and, give or take a few in between, ends it with an empty one. Buy ten or fifteen quid's worth of Four Star on a Saturday and you're bound to have some left in the tank at midnight. So some weeks I add a few miles, others I take a few off. If that's fiddling, I'm fiddling.' Bott 1, Management 0.

Another management 'assassin' asked one of our news reporters 'Your new company car okay?' 'Fine. Absolutely no complaints. Goes like a dream,' replied the hack. 'Well, I am surprised,' said the 'assassin', smugly 'because according to your expenses, it's only doing 3.5 miles to the gallon!'

And while I've got company cars on the brain, I'm reminded of another national paper scribe who went to his local garage, one of dubious reputation, and said 'Can you do something with the clock?' 'Sure, mate, want it winding back a few thousand miles?' 'Well, no. Actually I want it winding ON seven thousand because I'm way ahead on my mileage for the company and they want the car back next week!'

Ten out of ten for style goes to the Fleet Street veteran who, having been made redundant, was holding court in the wine bar adjacent to the office. A management flunky, who had latched on to the party, sniped 'You haven't yet returned your company car.' 'Sorry, old boy,' boomed the vet, with great effect. 'No can do. Gave it to the wife as part of the divorce settlement!'

One of the nationals had a staff man in Ireland years ago who charged mileage here, there and everywhere but never submitted a bill, for petrol, repairs, road tax anything. The news editor became so suspicious, he actually flew to Dublin one day and looked in the bloke's garage!

Another Dublin-based reporter on a national used to claim several times a year for boat trips to Ushers Island to cover stories or entertain contacts. No problem, until the day one of the London hierarchy paid an unexpected visit to Dublin office and got stuck in traffic on the way into the city from the airport. He looked out of the taxi on the quays and saw the street name Ushers Island.

I went round the world for the SEX (no, not that, the *Sunday Express!*) but I was never in the 'Champagne League, Premier Division' like some I could name but won't; never had the clout of Fleet Street legends like the war correspondent, with an ego to match his girth, who found the act of filling in an expenses claim such a distasteful exercise he kept the details to a bare minimum.

After weeks and months away among the muck and bullets, he returned to his London office and eventually submitted a claim which read only : 'To covering the Korean War: £5,000.' The editor called him into his office and said, almost apologetically 'Look, there is not a problem with the amount, old boy, but just for the sake of keeping the auditors and accountants happy, would you mind awfully itemising your claim?' The gnarled veteran of half a dozen campaigns grunted his indignance, retired to his desk before submitting a new claim form which read : 'Taxi to Victoria Station, twelve shillings and sixpence. To covering Korean War four thousand nine hundred and ninety nine pounds, seven shillings and sixpence.' He was recompensed in full.

Similarly, a famous sports reporter took his revenge on a typical piece of bureaucratic nit-picking. It was pointed out to him that the company's new policy for reporters travelling abroad to cover events had to be submitted ENTIRELY in the currency of that country. Having just returned from an England game in Moscow, he re-submitted a claim which began: 'Taxi to Heathrow, 15 roubles.'

Don Evans, that now-retired doyen of northern soccer writers and *News of the World* scribe who I am sure NEVER 'made an excuse and left', tells a lovely story about a BBC correspondent, working in eastern Europe during the 'cold war', who was suddenly taken to task by his superiors in London over his expenses. The correspondent received a telex querying his expenses claims over a lengthy period. 'For the past two years you have consistently claimed large amounts for paying and entertaining a Lt. Col. Ivan Popov, of the 23rd Hungarian Light Infantry, in exchange for information exclusively received. Our own investigations have revealed that not only is there no record of any such person as a Lt. Col. Ivan Popov but no 23rd Hungarian Light Infantry either.'

The message ended with the curt postcript 'Your observations would be welcomed by return.'

The foreign correspondent hit the 'bouncer' out of the ground with the admirable reply: 'Your revelations are much appreciated. I will never believe another word the man says!'

Similarly, at a time when the *Sunday People* were having a crackdown on expenses, a senior reporter was told by his editor 'I'd better have a word with you in private about yours.' 'No way ... I've got nothing to hide and if you've got something to say to me, you can say it in front of the rest of the staff.' 'Suit yourself. You have been charging entertaining and payments for tip-offs to a certain member of the House of Lords for several years?' 'What about it?', said the pompous hack. The editor replied 'He's been DEAD for 18 months!'

Foreign trips can be a licence to live like kings or queens, depending how the mood takes you and, of course, the gender. It's never much of a problem obtaining indecipherable bills, even if you have to write them yourselves. Try doing that in Tokyo or Peking? Don't get me wrong, there is a good deal of legitimate entertaining done on foreign trips ... expensive entertaining. But the average scribe's reputation for having hollow legs can be a disadvantage if something is lost in the translation.

After a splendid dinner somewhere in Germany, the meal accompanied by copious quantities of beer and wine, half a dozen members of the English press corps were presented with one fiercesome all-embracing bill instead of individual ones, a frequent occurrence.

'More bills, mein herr,' demanded one of our number. 'Jawol,' grinned our host and promptly pulled another six large foaming glasses of draught Pils.

On another England soccer trip, to the Turkish city of Izmir, there was a problem obtaining anything other than a printed receipt. Eventually, a national paper 'snapper' (photographer), with a reputation for greed, triumphantly produced a tatty blank bill bearing the name of a nearby bar/restaurant. He clutched it like a winning lottery ticket. Then, realising it needed some careful attention to be of real value, asked a Turkish journalist to write down 'two lunches and a couple of bottles of wine.' The Turk obliged—but took the request literally and wrote out the order in ENGLISH!

I admire the ingenuity shown by journalists in foreign fields and, when you think about it, often company money has to be spent in the most unlikely situations just to get from A to B. A foreign correspondent once claimed for 'buying a donkey' to get him across some impossible terrain. His office went along with it until later confronted by a further claim for 'loss on resale of donkey and hire of camel.'

A group of hacks, who loved a wager, were discussing eccies in a Fleet Street watering hole when one of the number boasted 'You can get away with anything if you are clever enough. Exes are money for old rope.' Immediately, he was challenged to do just that. Several weeks later, after a working trip to the Shetlands, his expenses sheet included a claim for 'old rope: £5'. When asked to explain, he told his news editor 'That rowing boat I hired to get across to one of the islands had nothing to secure it so I had to pay a bloke a few quid for a piece of old rope.' He got his expenses and won his bet.

A frustrated 'snapper', furious at having his expenses slashed week after week, wired his picture editor a photo from somewhere in Africa of an open-sided hut, just four poles and a roof made from twigs and leaves. It was accompanied by the sarcastic comment 'This is my hotel room. It's all I can afford under the new cuts!'

Quite the most outrageous expenses claim I ever heard about was for 'reverse mileage'. It was only when some eagle-eyed accountant at this particular national paper spotted it that the cheeky hack, a Yorkshire-based sports writer, received a memo saying 'We note that over a period of 18 months you have been paid a total of £245 for "reverse mileage". Please be kind enough to explain what is "reverse mileage"?' The scribe sent a memo by return, claiming

'My house has a very long drive and I calculate the amount of petrol I use each month to reverse out of it!'

Rumour has it that because he was such a tight bastard, when the office put the block on that particular little perk, he moved into a terraced house!

A colleague of mine, an eloquent raconteur was speaking at a dinner attended by numerous sporting celebrities, when he said mischievously 'It is indeed an honour to meet at long last so many of the people I have been entertaining to lunch over the past fifteen years!'

Expense accounts, in all manner of businesses and professions, can be a welcome perk. Some, who buy chip butties and claim for caviar, use them to line their pockets. I recall one who went as far as to design and print his own restaurant bills. But the majority are grateful to enjoy the lifestyle that goes with the job. After all, the hours can be pretty unsociable.

Alan Cave, who used to be the rugby league writer for the old *Daily Herald*, which became the *Sun*, called into the Manchester office on his day off to pick up his wages and answered an SOS. London had tipped them off that the Australian runner John Landy was in Dublin and was going to make an attempt on the world mile record at the Santry Stadium. There was a flap on because no one was available to cover the story. So Alan was asked to drop everything and fly over to Dublin, where all the arrangements would be taken care of.

Being an old pro, he got himself across to Dublin and covered the world record attempt, albeit an unsuccessful one. To add to his frustration, there wasn't an hotel bed to be had in the Irish capital and it was only with the help of a contact that he was able to kip down in the ballroom of the Gresham Hotel. Not before he had answered another late call from the office, to chase up a racing story about the Aga Khan selling his stud in Ireland—a tale which had surfaced in the early editions of one of his paper's rivals.

So the intrepid Alan managed only a couple of hours sleep on the ballroom carpet before he was heading back to

Manchester, unshaven, unkempt and with no change of clothing. The return flight from Dublin was delayed and then, halfway across the Irish Sea, developed an engine fault and had to return. Eventually, Alan landed in Manchester on a replacement aircraft and staggered into the *Sunday People* just in time to begin his Saturday night casual duty as a stone sub.

Unfortunately, one of the company's hierarchy chose that night to do a tour of the works and spotted Alan. You can more or less guess the rest. 'What's that dishevelled bastard doing working for this newspaper? If the man can't be bothered to wash or shave or turn in looking half decent, get rid of him.'

Most of us in journalism can relate to that situation—and this little postscript. The previous night, when John Landy was preparing for his world record attempt and Alan Cave was heading across the Irish Sea without so much as a toothbrush, Mrs Cave phoned the *Herald* sports desk and asked 'Have you seen Alan, his dinner is in the oven?'

Unsociable hours? You bet. I wonder what he put on his expenses sheet for those two hours on the ballroom carpet.

Never kill the goose that lays golden eggs. The *News of the World* are famous for exposing the 'wages of sin'—but what about their own? One of their investigators was asked to explain why he had claimed for paying a call girl £300 for 'personal services' when she was heard quite distinctly on the video to ask for only £200? 'Naturally I made an excuse and left—but I gave her a big tip!'

I suppose if there is an art to 'doing your eccies' it is the art of disguise, as illustrated by my final offering.

A Scottish sports writer once claimed for a new trilby hat after having his favourite titfer blown into the sea on a channel crossing. On his return he had a blazing row with his parsimonious sports editor, who refused to sanction the cost of a new hat. The following week, when the writer submitted his next expenses sheet, his boss scoured it with the proverbial fine tooth comb. 'Aye, these are ok. There's no hat this week, then?' The hack looked him straight in the eye and snarled 'It's there alright ... but you canna see it!'

Five

THE VROOM! YEARS

SPEEDWAY has come close to replacing football as my favourite spectator sport for a great chunk of my working life. I discovered it at Blackbird Road, Leicester, in the mid-Fifties when I spent the easter weekend with my aunt and uncle. I was dazzled by the chrome of the bikes, the speed, the noise, the dust, the smell, the raw excitement it all generated.

So when I left Harrogate, in December 1959, and joined the *Coventry Evening Telegraph*, the real bonus was being asked to cover speedway. It was the start of a great romance which, since I have never been remotely interested in any other form of motor cycle racing or even riding or owning one, is difficult to comprehend. Sprockets and rocker arms, gear ratios and cams, are still double Dutch to me but the characters, the cameraderie and the courage of the riders is beyond dispute.

Of course, they are all mad. Anybody who races on a tight, enclosed, oval-shaped circuit with a loose-dirt surface against three other riders on 500 cc motor bikes, with no brakes, has to be certified insane. They break their bones the way others break bread, get up and walk away after the most horrifying crashes and treat pain as a minor irritant. Fear, as we know it, doesn't seem to exist in their world.

Thankfully, accidents are not always as bad as they seem. I was in Los Angeles in 1982 for the World Championship Final and went to a meeting at Costa Mesa the previous night. The track was so small and there were so many crashes that Phil Rising, editor of the excellent *Speedway Star*, called it 'speedway skittles'. Four riders went down in a heap on one bend and for an awful moment I thought I saw a severed leg fly across the track. Then it was pointed out to me the rider in question had a wooden leg and it was 'always coming off'.

During my time as the Press Officer at Hull, one of our madcap Americans, Kelly Moran, had a spectacular crash at Hackney and was thrown unconscious into a flower bed on the centre green. When he came round and found himself lying on his back with flowers all around him, he thought he'd died and gone to heaven.

Others weren't so fortunate. Two of my favourite riders, good mates and England internationals, Alan Wilkinson and Joe Owen, are in wheelchairs for life and I have heard The Last Post sounded for others who have paid the ultimate price. Almost as sad is that speedway, which attracted huge crowds in the 30's and late 40's—aggregating nearly eleven million spectators in the 1948 season—has struggled to survive in the last two decades. Too many people USED to go to speedway, too many tracks fell by the wayside, too many 'foreigners' won the world championship and too many sports editors lost interest.

Shamefully, I went AWOL myself for a few years, retaining a slender link as Press Officer for the annual indoor ice meetings at Telford. My excuse is that my job description changed and speedway was not encouraged to be part of it until I had the opportunity to pick up the pieces again recently. Previously, for the best part of 30 years I went nearly everywhere. World finals at home, Wembley, White City and Bradford, abroad in Sweden, Denmark, Poland, Germany, Holland, America. European finals, British finals, Nordic, Overseas and Inter-continental finals, Test matches, testimonials, cup finals, open meetings, you name it. Even a day trip to Poland!

Wembley used to be the 'home' of the world championship final and speedway has never been quite the same since it all ended there in 1981. But at least we began to explore new frontiers. Holland is not a country generally associated with speedway yet there were few complaints from the press when the FIM decided to stage the world final in Amsterdam in 1987. The former British champion and England coach Eric Boocock joked 'Every time the red lights went on to stop a race, six hookers jumped on to the track!'

At various times I was the Press Officer at Nelson, Bradford, Doncaster, Newcastle, Hull (for 11 seasons) and Wembley Arena (for the five Lada indoor internationals), broadcast for BBC Radio Manchester, commentated for Yorkshire Television and Tyne-Tees, wrote 13 books, helped to organise a few testimonial meetings, chaired the Speedway Writers and Photographers Association for five years, penned a few hundred columns and reports and managed the business affairs of England's own world super star Peter Collins for eight years. So I was what you might say 'involved'. And relished every privileged minute.

I would love to see speedway enjoy another boom and not just because I am involved again.

It is always a privilege to meet and interview sporting legends and listening to characters like Johnnie S. Hoskins, the man who 'invented' speedway in Australia, back in 1923, Jack Parker, Dent Oliver, Frank Varey and Oliver Langton, made me wish I had been around in the cinder-track days. Can you believe some sports editors still think they race on cinders? Maybe you do, too.

Frank Varey, who was nick-named El Diablo Rojo (The Red Devil) by the Argentinians when he first rode there in 1929, because of his red jumper and reckless style, used to have me in stitches at Belle Vue when I was writing his life story for the *Manchester Evening News* in the early 70's. He told me about his legendary duels with Wembley's Australian star Lionel Van Praag, the first official world champion, in 1936, and how a 60,000 Wembley crowd wanted to lynch him after he had knocked off their hero.

'I wasn't hurt myself but I thought it safer to pretend I was,' recalled Frank. 'So I lay there on the track and the ambulance men carried both of us off on stretchers. Just as we reached the pits gate, I sat bolt upright and gave the crowd two fingers. I couldn't resist it. They went potty.

'Lionel and me used to scrap everywhere, on the track, in the pits, in the dressing room. The feud went on so long the Auto Cycle Union ordered us to call a truce and shake hands in the middle of Wembley Stadium. I think that was the night I knocked him off again.'

Frank told me about another memorable night when he captained England to an 'Ashes' victory against Australia at Belle Vue, in the hey day of the Manchester pleasure park, and what happened when the riders went to one of the crowded dance halls to celebrate. 'We were as popular as any international footballers in those days—earning more, too—and the manager was delighted to let us in free. I said we had an Australian with us and would they let him in, too? "No problem", said the dance hall boss. He didn't realise we'd borrowed a baby kangaroo from Belle Vue Zoo. It didn't half clear the dance floor quick. Hopping all over the place.'

One of Frank's tales was a bit gruesome. He recalled how another England international, 'Dusty' Haigh, lost a finger in Argentina in an accident while he was warming up his engine. 'He collapsed and they were just reviving him in the first-aid room when I walked in. I said "It's okay, 'Dusty', I've found your finger. Some ants were carrying it off to their nest like pall-bearers". Funny, he blacked out again at that point!'

Johnnie Hoskins, the pioneer and greatest of all speedway promoters, Barnum and Bailey rolled into one, lived to be 93. Well into his 70's he was still promoting, still a showman, still setting fire to his trilby hats. I phoned him at his clifftop home in Herne Bay late in 1973 when I was writing the Champions Book of Speedway No 5. 'Johnnie, will you write me a piece for my book about speedway's first fifty years?' He was 81 but the reply was instant, like a gunshot. 'How much are you paying, boy?'

In my first year of reporting speedway, 1960, I started travelling to the away meetings, either on the Coventry Bees supporters' trips or with one of the riders, Nick Nicholls. He gave me a lift to New Cross one night and it was my first experience of the recently-opened M1 motorway. Most speedway riders drive cars as if they are still on the track and Nick was no exception. I kept waiting for us to take off. But if that was scary, suddenly the bonnet of his Ford Zephyr (or was it a Zodiac?) shot up flat against the windscreen. We couldn't see a thing and we were doing about ninety five in the fast lane. Somehow, we got across to the hard shoulder without colliding with anything.

While I was looking for a change of underpants, Nick got his tool box out of the boot, hammered the buckled bonnet down as far as it would go, which was not far enough, and tied it to the radiator cap with a shoe-lace. Then he hit the fast lane again while I prayed that one good gust of wind wouldn't blow the bonnet up again. Why don't speedway riders worry about anything except points money?

They can be pretty temperamental. I've seen a few punch-ups in the pits over the years and some promoters used to drag the assailants out onto the track so the fans could enjoy it, too. Referees cop for most of the flak, which is one reason why they tend to sit in little boxes on the roof at the back of the stand. One rider was banned sine die for throwing a referee into the bath.

In the early 70's, when I was covering Belle Vue for the *Manchester Evening News*, the sports editor Vernon Addison asked me to get him a couple of stand tickets for a league match against Leicester because it was his young son's birthday and he had heard speedway was a sport for all the family. Which it is, normally. He just happened to pick a Saturday night when two riders, Alan Wilkinson and Alan Cowland, had a set-to on the track and a fan vaulted the fence and got involved. It was like lighting the blue touch paper. Suddenly, riders, mechanics and fans were going at each other hammer and tongs in the only mass brawl I have ever seen at a speedway track. Fortunately, the sports editor's news sense overcame any feelings of disillusionment. 'Bloody amazing ... you'd better write it up as the back-page lead for Monday. And we want to go again next week!'

My involvement with Peter Collins began when I was freelancing the first time round and he was just beginning to emerge as the brightest English star since his own hero, the late, lamented Peter Craven. I was lucky enough to see Craven win his second world title at Wembley in 1962, the year before he was killed in a track crash at Edinburgh. Collins, the eldest of five brothers from Cheshire who all became professional riders, was a natural-born racer who was destined to become world champion and should have won it more than once. Also I find it quite disgraceful that his ten world titles—one individual, four pairs and five team—plus 136 England appearances and more than 5,000 points for Belle Vue, have still not been rewarded with the MBE or OBE.

I may be biased but I believe that if winning ten world titles and leading England to three successive World Team Cup triumphs was not enough to merit an award, the man's heroism certainly was.

The year after he achieved his life's ambition, winning the world individual title in Poland, in 1976, he was a week away from defending it in Sweden when his leg was broken and almost amputated in a horrific accident at Belle Vue, his home track. A steel drain cover, just inside one of the bends, had been accidentally dislodged by a hosepipe while the track was being watered during the interval. Nobody noticed it was now protruding over the 'white line' ... until Collins hit it at full throttle making a sweep on the inside.

Collins was rushed to hospital in agony with a compound fracture of the fibula and severed muscles. Two hundred internal stitches and 32 external were required apart from attention to the fracture itself. Yet somehow, unbelievably, courageously, foolishly, Collins flew to Gothenburg just six days later and not only rode in the wettest world final of all time but finished runner-up!

He travelled by car, airport luggage trolley, Sir Charles Forte's private jet and his own van, went straight to the Ullevi Stadium, where he carried out his own track inspection on a mobile stretcher. He spent the entire meeting on crutches, when he wasn't being lifted on or off his four-valve Weslake machine, rode his heart out and lost his title to the 'king', Ivan Mauger— the only six-times individual champion in history.

Later he reflected 'I suppose I was crazy to even think about riding but if I was going to lose my title I wanted it to be on the track, not in a hospital bed. I was full of pain-killing tablets and felt ill all through the meeting but I made five good starts for once and nearly pulled it off. Better to lose my title than one of my legs.'

For me, Collins's show of courage on a near-waterlogged track in Gothenburg, in the cut-throat atmosphere of a 'sudden death' world final, was an even greater achievement than when he won in Katowice a year earlier. Where he was unlucky was in being world champion in the same year, 1976, as two rather more charismatic motor sport giants, James Hunt (motor racing) and Barry Sheene (motor cycling). Any other year and he would have been far more marketable.

The formation of SWAPA (Speedway Writers and Photographers Association) in 1978 was the start of properly-organised media trips to world finals. Even impoverished and oppressed Poland was more fun when we could fly to Berlin and charter a coach, laden with good food and drink, and drive east, although 'Checkpoint Charlie' was a pain.

On SWAPA's return from the 1986 world final in Katowice, we were stuck at the infamous checkpoint for hours and it did little for our humour after the long drive from Silesia. Some of us registered our own token protest against communism by relieving ourselves against the Berlin Wall. On the west side, needless to say. We weren't that brave!

In the days before lap-tops, notably in Poland, we sent our reports by telex because you could never be sure of getting telephone calls in or out of the country on the same day. I waited four hours for a call from the *Sunday Express* on one Polish jaunt and missed two editions. Then, by mistake, I was put through to the madhouse of the sports desk instead of the copy-takers. 'Richard Bott,' I said, preparing to dictate my story. 'Sorry, mate, he's not here tonight ... he's in Poland.' And the pillock put the phone down, cutting me off for another hour. Jesus Christ!

I know, for a fact, that other scribes have suffered an almost identical fate and been left fuming into the mouthpiece.

Harry Harris, the *Daily Mirror's* chief soccer writer, was on an England tour of Chile, Brazil and Uruguay and tried for days to get a call home to his wife. Eventually, he got through and the conversation sounded something like this to his colleagues 'Hello ... at last ... I've been trying to get a call out every time we've landed. It's been impossible. How are ....what? Yes, alright then ... .' And with that, Harry put down the phone, clearly exasperated. He turned to a couple of his fellow travellers and said 'How do you like that? It takes me a week to get through and she says can I ring back in ten minutes when Coronation Street has finished?'

Problems with getting the words back to the office were the bane of many a sports writer's life for years on foreign trips. Some calls were cut off within seconds, for no good reason. Imagine the frustration on the sports desk of the *Liverpool Echo* when their soccer man Michael Charters was reporting on an afternoon game from a stadium in the old soviet union. He had just managed to blurt out the words 'And the sensational news is that Liverpool ... ,' when the line went 'dead'.

On a couple of occasions, behind the old 'Iron Curtain', I crossed a receptionist's palm with silver and sneaked into the back of some grotty Polish hotel to type a telex myself on some antiquated machine. It was like being a linotype operator back at Ackrills or operating my mother's old foot-pedal sewing machine. Doubtless it was considerably worse for war correspondents. Just occasionally, their paths and circumstances intertwined.

The late Joe Humphreys, the *Daily Mirror's* rugby league reporter found himself and his colleagues caught up in war-torn Beirut en route to Australia to cover a Great Britain tour. Every foreign desk in London was trying to get a line through to the beleagured city, including the Mirror, when Joe's voice suddenly rang out on the copy desk. Professional to the last and seemingly oblivious to the mortar shells dropping all around him, he started dictating the real story 'Halifax are ready to make a sensational bid for the Widnes and Great Britain loose forward etc etc.'

When the copy-taker realised where Joe was phoning from and said 'Don't you know there's a bloody war going on?' He replied 'I thought it was a bit noisy!'

A more serious side to a similar situation befell another *Mirror* sports writer, Graham Baker, after England had won speedway's World Team Cup in Poland in 1980. Lech Walesa was leading the Solidarity revolt and it was a touchy subject with the commies. A group of us, on our way home from Wroclaw, missed the connecting flight in Warsaw, because of fog, and our visas had expired. It didn't do us any favours when Graham tried to file his report on the speedway from his hotel room and some bright spark on the *Mirror* news desk chipped in and said 'Never mind the bloody speedway, find out what you can about this revolt?'

It was no co-incidence that within seconds all our telephone lines went 'dead' and we were ordered to hand over our passports. Fear of being arrested and left to rot for months in some Polish nick prompted us to drain our minibars one by one. Come to think of it, we would have done anyway.

Apart from the journalistic involvement, I thoroughly enjoyed my decade as PRO at Hull. Ian Thomas is one of the best promoters and team managers in the business and our working relationship has continued through his indoor successes at Wembley Arena and Telford Ice Rink, the former in conjunction with world champions Ivan Mauger and Barry Briggs, the latter with former Hull and England rider Graham Drury.

Ian is a good friend and I don't think we have ever had a cross word in nearly 30 years. But he and his old sparring partner Brian Larner used to cause me some embarrassment with their practical jokes. I recall two instances at airports abroad, queuing at Passport Control where you are invariably confronted by someone who has had a sense-of-humour by-pass. It doesn't help when a raised voice behind you asks 'Are you still using your brother's passport, Dick?'

On another occasion, returning from some foreign trip with a fragile porcelain vase in a cardboard box tied with string, the curiosity of a silent queue was triggered by the remark 'I think it's cruel keeping a kitten inside a box with no ventilation.' It doesn't take much for imaginations to run riot and, before I could respond, people were berating me from all sides, prodding me with umbrellas and hitting me with handbags.

En route to Vojens, Ian and myself stopped for breakfast at Trowell motorway service station on the M1. At six in the morning the cafeteria was almost deserted and one of the cleaners was mopping the floor as we put down our trays of bacon and eggs. Waiting until the cleaner had her back to us, Ian said 'Don't hurt her, Dick, she's only a cleaner.' Then, as the woman turned in panic, he said to her 'It's alright love, he can't help it. They've only just let him out of the institution and he still has a few funny turns.' Next thing, the cleaner is pointing her mop at me and shouting 'Don't come near me, you loony.' Thanks, Ian.

When he re-introduced speedway to Workington in 1970, hundreds got in free to the first meeting by crossing the river behind Derwent Park 'tight-rope walking' the sewage pipe. He soon put a stop to that by smearing axle grease on the pipe the following week, with the obvious results. Thankfully, nobody drowned!

Workington had a local lad in their team called Steve Watson, who perfectly illustrates the extraordinary philosophy some riders have towards pain and injury. Ian recalls 'Steve was handicapped to start with because he had only one eye. And one night he came off and hit the fence so hard, I was convinced he was a gonna. I rushed over to him as he lay flat out on the track and as he started to come round, asked him how he felt. He just grinned at me and said "Bloody smashing ... it's the first time in my life I've had double vision!"

Ian was and still is always 'good for a story'. He could never understand promoters who responded to press calls by saying 'There's nothing doing'. The same dullards wondered why Ian's tracks enjoyed so much national paper publicity in the days when speedway could count on a few column inches. Look after the press and, for the most part, they'll look after you.

We laid on a press conference to launch the Lada cars tie-up with Newcastle Diamonds, already sponsors of Hull Vikings, in 1980, and encouraged questions by dressing up a buxom model in coloured balloons and very little else. Ask a question, pop a balloon. They came at us like machine-gun fire.

Lada also backed the indoor internationals at Wembley Arena from 1979 to 1983 inclusive. The racing was supplemented by a variety of interval entertainers, two of whom came close to being thrown out before they started. Amid the chaos of the preparations for the launch, on December 2 1979, a disbelieving Wembley security officer grabbed me in the pits area—very painful!—and said 'You the press officer? There's some bleedin' idiot out the back demanding to see yer, says his name is "Rhubarb". I've told 'im twice to piss orf?'

'No way,' I replied. 'Has he got his mate "Custard" with him?' The security officer thought I was some kind of nut. 'You're windin' me up and I 'aven't got time for any pissin' abaht.' Eventually, I convinced him that 'Rhubarb and Custard' were a pair of circus clowns we had booked as the interval attraction and just wanted to get their 'exploding car' into the pits.

An hour later, with a capacity crowd eager for the start of the first-ever indoor speedway international at Wembley, I stepped out into the spotlight in my dinner suit and dickie bow, roving microphone in hand, to introduce the 18 international riders. So, thanks to speedway, at least I can say I have something in common with legends like The Haarlem Globe Trotters, Diana Ross, Barry Manilow, The Rolling Stones and Elton John ... I've 'played' to a full house at Wembley!

Six

WHAT THE HELL?

ONE form of motor sport which leaves me cold is Stock Car Racing. But it was a good little earner for eight months a year when I first went free-lancing, in the late Sixties, and started working for speedway promoters. I used to knock out the programmes, advertising and press releases for multi-track promoter Mike Parker.

In those days, before the micro-chip changed the world, I used to type all the press releases and adverts on stencils and run them off on an old Gestetner printing machine that weighed a ton and invariably jammed every few minutes. It was like being a motor mechanic, trying to start the engine with a cranking handle. After half an hour there was more printing ink on me than on the paper.

The job filled me with about as much enthusiasm as stock car racing. All that banging and crashing, white tops, red, tops, blue tops, gold tops, like bloody milk bottles, did nothing for me. Nor did 'banger' racing which was even less sophisticated—but Mike made a pile out of it and I sensed a few possibilities myself after a while.

'Banger' racing is about adapting practically any old car—take out the glass, the trimmings and all but the driver's seat, put in cowguards and roll bars—to bump and grind round a track and give the punters a cheap thrill or two. Mike patented the name 'Hell Drivers' and used to advertise for up to 100 drivers a meeting to pay £1 each to enter. There was more glory than prize money for the winners so, effectively, they were paying to entertain the paying public. Not bad for the promoter, eh?

He did have to hire the stadiums, like Salford dog track, Manchester's White City, Nelson, Newcastle, Stoke, Silloth and Stanley, and the organisation and administration was very professional. A few Hell Drivers meetings developed into a Northern Championship and then a British Championship which it was my job to administrate as well as publicise.

We worked out a system of regional qualifying rounds and semi-finals, hyped up some of the characters and personalities into 'stars' and were never short of a write-up somewhere or even a spot on regional television. I found a few 'Jim'll- Fix-It' volunteers and a couple of young TV presenters daft enough to have a go. More publicity, bigger crowds. Any driver who kicked against the system and asked for appearance money or a bonus, after making a few headlines, was told to sling his hook.

Since I was the one who kept all the stats and biographies of the drivers, I reckoned, after a couple of years, a modest 'Hell Drivers Annual' might find a market and Mike said 'Go ahead and we'll sell it but it has to be at your own expense.'

I spent months putting this little paper-back job together, with photographs, biogs, results, fixtures and records and tried to fund it by getting the drivers to advertise in it. No problem, until I asked for payment. Some did, some didn't. I had 4,000 handbooks printed—a gamble—and they were ready for the start of the 1972 season. But Mike Parker wasn't.

White City opened to be followed in the next two weeks by Stoke, Stanley, Salford, Newcastle and Silloth. But on that first night, with a good crowd in, Mike said 'Sorry, can't spare anybody to sell those things because my people are busy selling programmes'. Charming. The only thing for it was to put on a white coat and walk round the track selling the bloody things myself. 'Get your 'ell drivers annual ... brand new this season ... all the facts and fixtures ... only 25p.'

My wife did the same and we managed to unload a few hundred copies between us before I had to chase round the pits interviewing drivers for copy for the next meeting, next programme, next press release. And because you have to strike while the iron is hot, as they say, we took the show on the road to the other tracks.

At one of them, Stanley, up in the north east, I had an embarrassing experience. I was hiding behind the white coat of anonymity when the track announcer blew my cover. There I was hustling, shouting 'Get your 'ell drivers annual ... only 25p' and answering any flak by blaming the price, the product etc on the promoter by saying 'I'm just selling them, mate' and 'yes, he is a greedy bastard.'

Suddenly, over the tannoy the announcer, trying to do me a favour, boomed 'On sale today we have the first-ever *Hell Drivers Annual* compiled and edited by Dick Bott ... and he's walking round selling it himself!' Thanks a bundle, Barry (Wallace). I'll forgive him because he's one of the best announcers in the business—the 'voice' at Brough Park and Newcastle United—but I didn't at the time.

I had done a bit of track announcing myself, when Mike Parker opened speedway at Doncaster in 1969. What a struggle! A tannoy that sounded like a strangled cat and curious supporters who didn't realise that speedway is about audience participation. The team were nick-named the 'Stallions' because of the town's horse-racing traditions. I remember a group of visiting Berwick supporters, a raucous lot, standing right in front of the announcer's box when I was trying to whip up a bit of enthusiasm for the home team. 'Give us an 'S', give us a 'T', give us an 'A', give us an 'L', give us another 'L' ... and so on ... ' The response was negligible. Then one of the Berwick fans pierced the silence around me. 'Don't know about Stallions, mate, but you're certainly flogging a dead 'orse!'

I felt about as popular as the German football fan who stands on the terraces at Borussia Moenchengladbach and shouts 'Give us a B'!

I had more fun as a track announcer when Mike Parker moved his Nelson Admirals set-up to Bradford's Odsal Stadium in the middle of the 1970 season and we opened to five-figure crowds. Announcing the results was hardly a problem with only four riders in a race. The problem with Stock Cars and 'bangers' was that after a few laps I never knew who was in front, who was at the back or what lap they were on.

In fairness to Stox as against 'bangers', it is a highly-organised sport with custom-built cars, very skilful drivers and a huge following. But it doesn't hold a candle to speedway for me.

There's one thing about speedway and stock car tracks you should know if you haven't been. They are not places for 'dressing up' unless you can be sure of being in a glass-fronted stand, bar or restaurant. My second wife, Sue, has still not forgiven me for taking her to Belle Vue for the first time years ago, in a long black dress and silver shoes. In fact, she would have been happier if I'd been wearing them!

Seven

TRAINS, PLANES AND AUTOMOBILES

TRANSPORT plays a major part in a sports writer's career although one of my best mates in national newspapers has never driven a car in his life. He says it would interfere with his social life too much. Instead of a garage and a drive he has a taxi rank.

Most of us are dependent on our 'wheels' as much as the trains, planes and other automobiles that take us from 'A' to 'B' in the call of duty. I have driven but not necessarily owned, everything from a three-wheeler Isetta bubble car to a Rolls Royce and guess in which one the distinguished former Wolves and England centre half Bill Slater was once my passenger?

A bubble car (circa 1960) had two wheels at the front, one at the back, a bench seat, left-hand drive, opened at the front like an escape hatch in a submarine and no reverse gear if, as in my case, you only had a motor cycle licence. Bill Slater accepted a lift home in 'the flying egg' after the Wolverhampton Wanderers team coach had returned late from a night match at Blackburn in the early 60's. By then I was covering Wolves, home and away, for the *Birmingham Evening Despatch* and the *Sports Argus*, and in my element. They might have been the least important of the First Division clubs in the west midlands, from the point of view of our circulation area, but they were also the most successful.

Bill was a true gentleman. There were none of the snide remarks about my bubble car I was used to hearing. 'Does it go forwards, backwards or up?' 'Do you keep it in an eggcup?'

Amazingly, it was stolen from outside a Birmingham city centre pub on my stag night in 1962. The police thought it was hysterical. 'You're kidding us, aren't you ... you've got it in your pocket!'

The 'local' press travelled with Wolves to away games, by team coach or train, or both. The legendary Stan Cullis was still their manager and he ruled with a rod of iron. On a trip to play Arsenal at Highbury, Cullis was still seething about a heavy defeat at Blackpool the previous week. So when the Wolves team coach began the descent of Highbury Hill to the Arsenal ground, Cullis ordered the coach to stop and made the players walk the last few hundred yards to stretch their legs. Imagine the faces of the crowd gathered by the main entrance when the coach pulled up, 'Wolverhampton Wanderers FC' clearly displayed in the front window, with only Cullis, his sponge man, three pressmen and five or six directors on board.

Travelling on the team coach can create problems. Often you are privy to remarks and incidents that may be newsworthy but the club would not want reported. Do you risk being banned from the coach for the sake of one juicy headline? And is it fair to give a bad write-up to a player who has been your card school partner en route to the game?

I had a season and a half travelling with Doncaster Rovers after being made redundant in Birmingham by the closure of the *Evening Despatch* in April 1963. They seemed to expect their local reporter to praise them from the rooftops when they won and go easy on the criticism when they lost or played badly. I couldn't operate that way and the relationship became strained when they had a string of bad results and, inevitably, strong criticism.

So, after a night match at Hartlepool, where Rovers lost again, played crap and stopped for a consolation drink at some pub out in the wilds of north Yorkshire, they very kindly left me behind. The coach pulled out while I was in the 'Gents'.

Safer to travel independently.

In my schooldays I had been transported to matches in cars, vans, lorries, trolley-buses, trams, the London underground, even a motor cycle and sidecar. Arguably the most uncomfortable were the Samuel Ledgard 'rattlers', blue double-decker buses that had hard, slatted wooden seats and jarred every bone in my body on each of the 18 miles from Harrogate to Bradford in the days when I followed the fortunes of Bradford Park Avenue. If you didn't suffer from vibrating piles when you got on, you did by the time you got off.

You could measure my progress in journalism by the transport I owned; a Raleigh pushbike on the *Harrogate Advertiser*, a Lambretta scooter on the *Coventry Evening Telegraph* and an Isetta bubble car on the *Birmingham Evening Despatch*. All second-hand, of course. Clearly, I still had some way to go.

I bought the bubble car after being knocked off my scooter—by a Robin Reliant, that other three-wheeled terror of the highways. The driver suddenly did a u-turn and I learned to fly in about five seconds flat. No real damage done. And ANOTHER let-off.

A month or so earlier I had been on my way to an FA Cup first round tie at Worcester, on the Lambretta. The throttle jammed wide open as I levelled out after going up a big hill. There I was, heading for traffic lights and a busy town centre like Evel Knievel. I couldn't change gear when I was accelerating and honestly didn't know what would happen if I switched off the ignition. I feared the machine would stall and launch me into orbit like a human cannonball. Thankfully it didn't but I suppose it was the closest I came to being a speedway rider or a stuntman.

Now that I have been driving cars and having them nicked, periodically, for thirty-odd years, I'm always amazed they are still where I left them in all manner of strange towns, cities and countries. 'Mind your car, mister?' is an offer you refuse at your peril in Liverpool. As the joke goes: 'No thanks, I've got a

Rottweiler in the boot'. 'Can it put out fires, mister?'

I had a *Sunday Express* company Ford Cortina stolen from outside our Manchester office—Ancoats, where they have broken glass for carpets—and it was missing for seven weeks. Eventually, it was recovered, with false number plates, in Preston. Not too badly damaged either, but it needed a good valeting to get rid of the muck and rubbish and some chunky pieces of glass I found lodged under the passenger seat. Later I learned the car had been picked up after a diamonds snatch at a jewellers in Southport. On reflection all my window glass had been intact. You're not thinking what I'm thinking, are you? If you had my luck, you'd come third in a duel.

I hired a car in Valencia when I was covering the 1982 World Cup Finals in Spain. It was just after the end of the Falklands War when the English were about as popular with the Argentines as a member of the Ku Klux Klan in Haarlem. I was covering Northern Ireland's group but decided to drive down to Alicante to watch Argentina play Hungary, just to see their new star, Diego Maradona, 'in the flesh'.

Absolutely no sweat, until my hire car stalled at traffic lights after the game in an area of Alicante where thousands of Argies were celebrating a 4-1 victory. Suddenly, it didn't seem the best place to ask for a push in an English accent! Maybe I should have had my 'survival kit phrase-book' with me. A colleague had given me three key phrases to use in such a crisis.

Whether they bore any resemblance to text-book Spanish was highly unlikely but they were, together with a rough translation, something like the following:

(1) *'No este muerco castrato, por favor'* *(please let go of my bollocks, you are torturing me).*

(2) *'Hablado usted contente que mucho Grand Malvenas'* *(I have told you before, you can have the bloody Falklands).*

(3) *'Si, comprende, no pata pata donde para Maradona, gola bueno'* *(I agree it was a perfectly good goal).*

I don't pray often but I did then and just when they were starting to beat their fists on the window, the little Seat engine restarted.

Occasionally, the true fan in me expresses itself. The passion, the anger or the elation. Scotland-England internationals used to turn some press men into worse hooligans than the terrace loonies. Games between the 'auld enemies' never bothered me that much until the Scots started winding me up—particularly when they beat us at Wembley. So, after England's 1-0 win at Hampden Park, in May 1982 (Paul Mariner scored), I was quite ecstatic.

It is well-nigh impossible to get back to Manchester from Glasgow on a Saturday night except by car. If you are working for a good hour and a half after the game, you have no chance of making the last train or flight—unless the time-tables have improved since the late 80's. So, the job done, myself and two other Manchester-based Sunday paper reporters, Don Evans and Norman Wynne, set off by car back towards the A74.

Don was driving, I was the back-seat passenger, needing a drink to celebrate England's win but sufficiently intoxicated by the result. As we motored round the Glasgow ring road, we passed a group of desolate Jocks, all drooping flags and banners and lurching from off licence to off licence. I couldn't resist it. I wound the window down and jeered 'See you Jimmy, we gave you a right stuffing today!' Almost immediately, the car slowed and came to a halt. 'Bloody hell, Don, why have you stopped?' 'Because the lights are on red.'

By now, so were the Jocks, sensing their chance to skin the hide of an arrogant Sassanach. The yellow streak down my back was widening by the second as they closed the gap to the stationary car. I had a quick look, saw we had nothing in front of us and screamed at Don 'If you CAN go, GO!!' Like a good ex-naval man, who was in minesweepers during the war, he quickly realised the predicament I had landed US in ... and shot through the lights. Sorry Scotland—and Don—it won't happen again.

The Rolls Royce I drove belonged to my speedway promoter pal Ian Thomas, who had a bizarre experience himself driving back alone from Barrow to his home in Yorkshire after an end-of-season meeting. The riders had doused him in flour and water and he had forgotten to take a change of clothing. Soaked to the skin, he set off back through the Lake District, stripped to his vest and underpants ... in the Roller!

'Just my luck ... the police flagged me down for a spot check,' he told me later. 'Imagine the look on this copper's face when he saw my state of undress and the look on mine when he asked "Okay, where's the bird?" I said there wasn't one. He insisted on looking in the boot and found a bag with a few thousand quid in it—the night's takings. I had some explaining to do, I can tell you.' That was one story he didn't give to the press.

My introduction to driving that 'Roller' was at East Midlands Airport at about three in the morning, on the way home from a speedway meeting in Denmark. I had never driven an automatic before, never mind a 'Roller'. Ian wasn't interested in excuses. He just got into the front passenger seat, reclined it and said 'I'm knackered, you're driving, wake me up when we get to Bradford.'

I seem to have spent half my life driving home from somewhere and a year or two ago, I discovered that it doesn't ALWAYS pay to tell the truth to the police. On many a trip abroad, with England, Manchester United, Liverpool etc, you fly back straight after the game and then have to drive home from Luton, Ringway or Speke and get home in the early hours of the morning. I was nearly home from one such trip when I was flagged down by the police on the outskirts of Rochdale at about three in the morning. They were on the look-out for somebody.

'Just a quick check, sir,' said the constable. 'Can you tell me where you are heading?' 'Smithy Bridge,' I replied, naming my village which was about a mile up the road. 'And where have you come from, sir?' 'Bratislava.' 'Heh, Serge, we've got a right bloody smart arse 'ere!' I got the 'third degree' for the next half an hour. Blow in the bag, number plate check, headlights, sidelights, tyres, tax disc. Why didn't I just say 'Salford'?

Taxis have been ferrying journalists round towns and cities for decades and since we are usually in a hurry to catch a train, a flight, a kick-off or 'last orders', we don't like being 'taken for a ride' when it comes to the fare or a roundabout route or both. Nice story about Bob Cass, of the *Mail on Sunday*, and a round-the-houses trip in London which Bob felt could have been completed in half the time.

Eventually, the taxi reached the requested destination and the driver, who had been piping 50's pop music into the back of the cab, said 'Ere you are, mate. That'll be eleven quid. And by the way, do yer recognise this little number? None of yer bang, bang, modern stuff in this cab. That's Ruby Murray singing Softly, Softly.' 'I know,' said Bob 'and when we got in this cab it was still at No 1!'

Trains are okay unless you have been to a major piss-up lunch and you are on the five o'clock from London Euston back to Manchester Piccadilly, when everyone else is stone-cold sober. I still wonder what happened to the plastic cup of black coffee that disappeared from my hand in the buffet car when I was trying to stand up on that 'wobbly bit' between carriages. One second it was there, the next my right hand was cradling fresh air. Since no one screamed from the effects of being scalded, I have to presume the cup and contents went out through an open window. I consoled myself with the fact that I was on the right train.

Newspaper offices are a fund of stories about reporters and subs waking up in Stranraer instead of Southend or some anonymous railway siding after boarding the wrong train, invariably after the Christmas 'do'.

Occasionally, if I was covering a Test match in London and left Lord's or The Oval so late on a Saturday I had to wait for the 'sleeper' to Manchester, I shared a nightcap or two with some northern-based production men who travelled back late on a Saturday night after their shift on the *Sunday Mirror* sports desk. Once under way, we used to torment the drunks who were shoe-horned into the 'cattle trucks' next to the First Class 'sleeper' coach. We would raise our miniatures in salute and they would try to kick the door in. Very brave, weren't we?

Mobile phones and BT phone card kiosks mean journalists and business people in general can now keep in constant touch with their head offices from the train. How sad. Come back with me to the good old days before these talking bricks were invented when, for a couple of hours or so, you could escape from work. Or try to.

There is a story about a rather naive young chap who was a part-time rugby union reporter for *The Observer* in the 50's, when railway carriages were divided into individual compartments. No phone cards, no mobile phones. Our hero had come up north to cover a game, telephoned his lengthy and lyrical report from Broughton Park and just managed to buy a *Manchester Evening News* PINK at Piccadilly before catching the last 'through train' back to Euston, with seconds to spare.

He sank into his seat, breathless but jubilant. Good match, good report, sorted. The train had just passed through Stockport, the last port of call before Euston, when he glanced at the PINK, found a report of the Broughton Park game and learned, to his horror that he had got the result wrong. A late score he thought valid had actually been disallowed, making a considerable difference to the final outcome. He spent the rest of the journey, panic-stricken, throwing scribbled notes showing the correct score out of the window as the train passed through station after station, with the plea: 'SOS. Emergency. Will someone please phone *The Observer* urgently with this message.'

I know the feeling. Together with some northern colleagues I travelled back north from Wembley, after the 1977 FA Cup Final (Manchester United 2 Liverpool 1), on Liverpool's chartered executive special, from Watford to Lime Street. We had been told that, win or lose, Liverpool would be making an early exit from Wembley because they had to prepare for the European Cup final against Borussia Moenchengladbach in Rome the following Wednesday. If we wanted to be sure of after-match quotes, we had to be on that train.

Fine. And when Liverpool chief executive Peter Robinson generously dropped a story in our laps that Kevin Keegan was heading for Hamburg for transfer talks after Rome, even finer. The only frustration was that it was a non-stop train. But, if we arrived on schedule at 10.15pm, there was plenty of time to catch the later editions of the 'Sundays'. Unfortunately, there were so many 'Supporters Specials' queuing up to get into Lime Street that it was after midnight before we pulled in and by then we were close to apoplexy.

A mobile phone would have been a godsend in that situation and many a time I have been thankful for having one with me. It's when they make you the prisoner of phone-aholic sports editors, you just want to dunk them in a barrel of water. Who wants to spend the entire journey from London to Manchester on the damned things?

One blessing is that there are so many overhead lines, steep embankments and tunnels on that route that mobile phones frequently cut out mid-conversation. The other ruse is to create your own 'interference' by making crackling noises into the mouthpiece, like that TV commercial where the chef pretends to be percolating coffee. It works a treat, I can assure you. A few of those and your boss will say 'Oh, forget it ... ring me when you get to Euston!' Heaven.

Not that you get any real peace because the suit-and-briefcase army are at it non-stop, chattering away like demented parrots. They get on and off trains with their mobiles clamped to their ears and their bleepers bleeping and you wonder how they ever coped without them. Thankfully they don't seem to work too well at 35,000 feet or, if they do, they're banned.

Plane trips can be flights of fancy, extraordinarily productive, sheer drudgery or a mite scary. The best have been to places like Australia, New Zealand, Malaysia and America with England's footballers, and with Liverpool, en route to and from European successes; the worst, several dodgy trips to Poland and an eventful flight to Denmark in a ten-seater Cessna.

The Cessna experience (sounds like the title of a Len Deighton thriller) was in the summer of 1980, when England became the first nation to achieve speedway's 'Grand Slam', winning all three world titles—individual, pairs and team. Anticipating the possibility, I went virtually everywhere that season, collecting interviews and background stories for a 'Grand Slam' book, in collaboration with my good pals and England team managers Ian Thomas and Eric Boocock.

So when they chartered a Cessna for the trip to the World Team Cup semi-final in Denmark, I was given the spare seat when one of the riders, Michael Lee, chose to go by boat. It remains the first and only time I have flown in a really small passenger aircraft since I've never been into crop-spraying.

We flew from East Midlands Airport, loaded up with packed lunches and a little liquid refreshment, and any fears and inhibitions I had soon disappeared as we cruised in a flawless blue sky at around 10,000 feet. One of our number was Ian's co-promoter at Hull, the extrovert Brian Larner. We were not far short of the Danish coast, when he sweet-talked the pilot into letting him handle the controls after feigning ignorance and showing genuine interest in the art of flying.

The pilot, a total stranger to all of us, fell for the three-card trick. 'How do you make it go up and down?' asked Brian, like a bashful schoolboy. The pilot demonstrated, gently easing the controls backwards and forwards. 'You can try it yourself, if you like!'

'You mean like THIS,' said Brian, throwing the plane into a steep dive. The bloody Red Baron was on the loose. Suddenly, the cabin was full of flying salad—two of the riders were eating their packed lunches—while the pilot struggled to save us from plunging into the North Sea. I don't know who got the biggest bollocking, Brian from the pilot, or the pilot from Danish air traffic control.

Actually, when we arrived in Denmark it was 'closed'! We landed at Esbjerg so early in the morning that the terminal building was locked. Our pilot walked round it knocking on the glass for nearly half an hour before he got a response.

The strangest noise I ever heard on an aircraft was the sound of empty bottles and cans rolling to the front of Liverpool's official team charter as it began the descent into Speke Airport after their first European Champions Cup triumph, in Rome in 1977. What a party that had been, starting at the final whistle and following with a lavish banquet in the Holiday Inn, when generously the club allowed scores of fans to join in. Sometime, in the early hours, I sat interviewing Jimmy Case in the near-deserted restaurant when a brandy bottle rolled out from under the table, followed by a hand which retrieved it.

Many a feature interview has been done or a 'hard' news story discovered on a return flight. That particular trip was made even more rewarding for me when I dropped on a rather good Tommy Smith 'exclusive'. It was on Manchester United's flight back from Barcelona in 1984 that the 'Sunday men' got Ron Atkinson to admit that if Bryan Robson wanted to go abroad the 'asking price' was £3 million.

Vince Wilson, a good pal from the Sunday Mirror, had the misfortune to suffer excruciating earache when a plane began its descent. On a trip home from the continent with Everton we waited patiently to grab a few minutes with Goodison boss Gordon Lee, in the hope of a good 'Sunday line'. Ten minutes out of Speke he sat down between us and was just about to 'cough' a transfer story when Vince went 'deaf'. Fortunately, my ears were okay and I clocked the story but the expression on Vince's face was priceless.

There have been sing-songs, parties, practical jokes and punch-ups on team flights since time immemorial and it is a shame that in today's world, there is nothing like the same camaraderie or trust. Or, because clubs and national associations tend to fill the aircraft to capacity, the same opportunities to fraternise.

I have had a few nightmarish flights, including Liverpool's 'near miss' descending into Warsaw in snow and fog in March 1983, en route to play Widzew Lodz in the European Cup. That could so easily have been another Munich! On a speedway trip to Poland, the pilot came down in fog when he was trying to 'find' Katowice and nearly hit a church.

The worst was a day-trip to the 1973 world speedway final in an old twin-engine Vanguard full of supporters. The flight from Luton to Krakow was fine but when we tried to take off on the return journey, the electrics failed. The pilot aborted two more attempts, then taxied back to the terminal. But it seems we had officially 'left the country' as far as the Poles were concerned, because it was past midnight and we had exceeded our time allowance.

Normally, in worrying situations, the pilot's cultured, reassuring English voice is like a soothing balm. But OUR pilot was from Wolverhampton and it did little for our peace of mind when he came on the tannoy and said 'Sorry about this, loik, but we seem to 'ave a bit of a problem. The loights won't wurk and the Powles won't let oos back into the turminal, cos they siy we've left the cuntry, loik. We'll just 'ave to sit 'ere 'til morning and troy agen in day-loight. Trooble is, these engines are bloody 'ard to get gowin' when they're cowd!'

And there we sat, with no air conditioning, until daybreak, scared shitless and wondering if the old crate would get off the ground. To be honest, I think the accumulative effect of more than a hundred and fifty passengers breaking wind simultaneously lifted us off that runway.

Eight

SOUND AND VISION

OBVIOUSLY, when you have dabbled a bit in radio and television commentating and reporting, you have a much greater appreciation of the professionalism of the Ken Wolstenholmes, John Motsons, Martin Tylers, Alan Greens and Desmond Lynams of the tranny and the magic lantern.

I use the word 'obviously' because it seems to be some sort of code word in radio and television interviewing, a prefix to almost every question and answer. And Peter Beardsley's mimics wouldn't be without it.

There must be some sort of bonus system based on the wretched word, maybe a fiver for every mention, which probably explains why it is much more prevalent in local radio and that fount of all knowledge 'Clubcall'! Obviously the network folk don't need the extra money.

They get enough stick, don't they? Motty and the others. It is easy to ridicule the people at the sharp end, a la 'Colemanballs', but generally they are the ones who manage to keep their heads when so many around them are losing theirs.

I had contributed to *BBC* local radio programmes, occasionally network, for a number of years before *Yorkshire Television's* Head of Sport Laurie Higgins heard me doing a radio commentary at Wembley, at a world speedway final, and invited me to have a crack at television. That consequently led to an offer from George Taylor, then in charge of sport at *Tyne Tees*. And I fronted a few meetings from Newcastle's Brough Park Stadium.

I'll tell you something, radio is a doddle by comparison. Most of the time, with radio, you see and you talk, just you and the microphone or a link into a programme. In TV, in my few years as a speedway commentator, there was always that third dimension—the director's voice in your ear. And the need to talk about what the VIEWER was seeing, not what you were. 'Watch the bloody monitor,' screamed the director from the control van, more often than not. After one such instance I shouted back (off air, of course) 'I can't even see it when I'm leaning out of this crappy press box trying to follow the race ... and, anyway, it's in black and white!'

Imagine what it must have been like for the television pioneers, even for Ken Wolstenholme in the days before colour monitors and action replays, climbing up ladders to some God-forsaken gantry with the wind howling up your cavalry twills. I don't envy today's commentators and I could never be one of those 'eye in the sky' cameramen stuck up at the top of a hydraulic lift at Wembley or The Open. What does he do if he gets taken short?

Personally, I could never maintain my concentration when, in the middle of a race, the director was rollicking the cameraman on the pits bend or his lady assistant was filing her finger nails or making idle gossip about who was 'shagging' who back at the studio.

The horse racing commentators are geniuses and the guys who commentate at big soccer tournaments like the World Cup and the European Championships also have my utmost admiration. Crowded fixture list. Unpronounceable names. *Yorkshire Television's* John Helm tells a story about a commentator who was struggling to get to grips with so many similar-sounding four-syllable foreign names in one such tournament and before commentators had the benefit of action replays from every angle. The matches were coming thick and fast and the commentary team were feeling the pressure. Too much travelling, too little sleep.

I think the match was Romania v Bulgaria. Suddenly, the Romanians scrambled a goal amid utter confusion. In desperation the commentator turned to his summariser and asked 'Who scored?' 'Fucked if I know', came the reply. Relieved, the commentator gasped on air 'And with 23 minutes gone it's Fuktifino for Romania. One-nil'.

Reg Gutteridge, one of the great boxing writers and TV commentators, used to contribute to the *Sunday Express* and always livened up our social events. He did a wonderful parody of *This is your Life* when the two Peter Watsons retired as our sports editor. I say 'two' because he could be charm personified or an absolute bastard depending how the mood took him.

One of my favourite stories about Reg is that he once sat between two of the all-time greats of heavyweight boxing at a dinner when they were arguing about who had the higher pain threshold.

Reg listened for a while, then said 'I've got a pretty high pain threshold myself' and promptly took his dinner fork and impaled it in his leg just below the knee, without so much as a flicker of reaction. The two heavyweights were speechless. They didn't know Reg had a wooden leg! He lost a leg in combat during the war and used to say he was the only press man who went for a night out on a trip abroad and tried to get his 'log' over.

I was always more comfortable with radio, apart from when England lost speedway's World Team Cup to the Danes in Landshut, Germany, in 1978, and I got my y-fronts in a twist. It was one of those typically spartan German tracks somewhere out in the Bavarian sticks. Somebody had locked the door of the chicken shed they called a press room and gone off to watch the last few races. So when, eventually, I got my phone call and was fed into *BBC Radio Manchester's* Saturday night requests programme, live, I blurted 'It's been a sod and sarry night for British speedway ... '

That was before mobile phones and covering events like the British Speedway Championship at Coventry was nothing but hassle. There were two phone lines plus a public phone near the pits and another half a mile down the road. One year I won the race to the only public phone in the main stand area, immediately after the riders had crossed the line in heat twenty. I called up *BBC Radio Manchester* only to be kept waiting for my cue until they finished playing a record. So by the time I began my 'live' report, some agitated Halifax Dukes fan was hammering on the door of the kiosk shouting 'How much bloody longer?'

In mid-broadcast, I put my hand over the mouthpiece, momentarily, told him to 'piss off' and continued to tell Mancunians how their boys had fared in the British Final. I like to think I did adjust to the needs of radio and TV better than some newspaper journalists and even the 'staffers' and expert summarisers are prone to dropping a clanger or three.

* Example 1: Commentator: 'Today Tranmere are playing with a five-man back four'.

Example 2: Commentator: 'The ball may have been going wide but it was a great shot on target'.

Example 3: Brian Moore : 'The whistle's gone, with Ray Houghton clearly four or five yards offside' . Ron Atkinson (summarising): 'For me that's when he's at his most dangerous!'

Newspaper reporters are often roped in to cover football or cricket for their local radio station, sometimes with limited experience and guidance. Take the national paper hack who had an interesting introduction to local radio in his younger days. He was asked to report on an FA Cup tie from a ground in the north east and was not aware it was customary for each reporter to give a 'weather check and pitch condition' on his first 'live' link. So when the studio presenter asked, on air: 'What's the weather like at Feethams, Bob?' the instant reply was 'It's bloody pissing down.'

* PRIVATE EYE COLMANBALLS 6 (CORGI BOOKS, 1994)

Another scribe, with absolutely no idea of what 'live' broadcasting entailed, went on air as if he was dictating to his newspaper's copy-takers. 'Darlington, comma, who were forced to make two late changes, comma, went a goal down after only four minutes, full point, new paragraph ... '

Sometimes the local radio guys are so overworked they forget to alert the studio or another programme presenter about what's on the schedule. I had to make a transfer charge call to *BBC Radio Manchester* from a big speedway meeting abroad one night, using the direct line number into the studio. They had a new presenter on and when the operator asked him to accept the charge, I heard him say 'Richard Bott? Never heard of him. Can't accept it.'

Another time, I had a tape ready for the early-morning news and the arrangement was for me to drop it off at the studios in Oxford Road when I got back from a big meeting in London. It was about three in the morning. Don't ask me where the night duty commissionaire was because I was hurling coins at windows for more than half an hour.

Tom Tyrrell is one of the characters of local radio—a voice synonymous with Manchester United and *Piccadilly Radio*. Good operator, regular guy, knows everybody and has helped me out a time or two with some United info. But Tom can be good for a chuckle when he gets a bit too cute.

He was about to record a one-to-one interview with manager Ron Atkinson after United had drawn a game at Ipswich. Tom started 'Well, Ron, you must be disappointed to drop a point after leading the game for an hour.'

Ron, who never liked to be pre-empted, put his hand over the microphone 'sponge' and said, sternly 'Disappointed? What to do you mean disappointed? Ipswich have gone ten games without defeat and we had three key players missing and one injured in the first half today. Disappointed? I'm bloody delighted ... You'd better start this interview again.'

Tom made the mistake of trying to be smart. So he re-opened with 'Well, Ron, you must be delighted to be going home with a point after going in against a form team without three key players.' Quick as a flash, Ron Atkinson responded 'Not really. To be honest, Tom, I'm a bit disappointed ... '

BBC Sports Report would never be the same without a match report delivered in the uniquely outrageous and colourful style of the amazing Stuart Hall. The man whose bubbling personality and infectious laugh did so much to popularise the TV series It's a Knock-out, paints mental pictures of knights in armour, jousting and pageantry or likens the players to Dickensian characters. Or whatever takes his mood. In the days when he had to sit in the old press interview room at Old Trafford and wait for his cue to go 'live' on air, the managers often had to stop in mid-session and wait until Stuart had finished.

I recall one game when Stuart launched into his epic and Ron Atkinson stood silently with the rest of us. As soon as Stuart had finished, Ron gave him a hug and said 'That was the biggest load of crap I've ever heard!'

You just can't dislike the guy. He is walking sunshine. Here's a comparatively recent gem from the Hall archives: 'Barmby stood out like a Pamela Anderson in a sea of Clair Rayners'. And another. Stuart was at Oldham's Boundary Park for a game against Ipswich and I heard him interview the Latics central defender Steve Redmond, the big-hearted Scouser who used to be with Manchester City. 'Steve, my boy,' gushed Stuart, 'in my report I have just described the Oldham defence today as pusillanimous. Wouldn't you agree?'

Well, I suppose he had to.

Nine

'COPY, PLEASE!'

SADLY, that urgent cry uttered by journalists the world over is in danger of disappearing from the language. This is an age of high technology when speed is of the essence and 'direct input' means stories are transmitted from lap-top PC's to editorial screens in seconds.

Copy-takers, that mysterious race of faceless men and women who have provided a link, often a buffer, between reporter and back bench for years, are being swept towards oblivion in the revolution.

In the same way that grieving printers bemoan the passing of Fleet Street and call it 'The lost city of the inkies', so the epitaphs are being prepared for the copy-taking fraternity. Is the fun going out of the game completely? Or is it a form of masochism we think is fun?

For every charming, quicksilver copy-taker, of either sex, who never asks you to spell words of one syllable and has the patience of Job while you punctuate every sentence with 'er' or 'um', there seem to be entire tribes of cynics and 'psychopaths' who hate and despise us more than their own mothers in law.

'*Sunday Express* copy? Hello, mate, it's Richard Bott with a Manchester United rewrite (the considered piece, with quotes, which follows the early on-the-whistle match report).' Silence ... then the knife-thrust. 'Why's that then? Couldn't you get it right the first time?'

After a few paragraphs, the yawns and sighs begin, closely followed by 'Is there much more of this crap?' A favourite ploy to torment the writer is to demand the same name is spelled out time after time or, even worse, to take issue with the copy. 'Isn't that the wrong tense? Don't you really mean inappropriate? You'd better give me this para again from the top because it doesn't make any sense to me?' They say that when they KNOW bloody well you are ad-libbing and can't remember the last word, never mind the last sentence!

Revenge is to throw in a word like 'existentialism'. They would never dare ask you to spell that. It would be a sign of weakness. Unless the weakness is on your part. Sub editors are the other enemy waiting to ambush the writer at every turn.

A *Birmingham Post* scribe went on to the subs after dictating a piece about David Platt moving to Italy and said 'I used the word Machiavellian ... would you mind checking the spelling for me?' The sub-editor responded, snidely 'How can I do that, then? Is he the president of Bari or something?' *

Occasionally, copy-takers and sub-editors are genuinely on a higher intellectual plane. A bright young *Sun* soccer writer 'doubled up' one Saturday by taking an order to cover the same match for the *Sunday Times* and had just begun dictating his report when the copy-taker said 'I say, old boy, I can't seem to spot a transitive verb in this first paragraph'. At which point, the reporter put his hand over the mouthpiece, turned in panic to a tabloid colleague and said 'What the f*** is a transitive verb?'

A *Daily Star* reporter caused a few titters when he was covering a match at Cambridge United in the early 80's. Cambridge had a young newcomer called Tom Finney and when the namesake of the legendary 'Preston plumber' scored the winning goal, the reporter said 'That'll do for me', went straight on to sports copy and began his report 'Cambridge triumphed with a goal from a player with an unforgettable name ... Alan Finney ... .er, sorry, Tom.'

Good, professional get-you-out-of-the-shit subs are worth their weight in gold. So are good copy-takers. I would accept I was the sole cause of their chagrin, frustration and bitterness if

* UMBRO BOOK OF FOOTBALL QUOTATIONS (STANLEY PAUL, 1993)

there were not so many examples of copy-taking confrontations, clangers, misunderstandings, etc.

Inevitably, there have been countless instances when the copy-taker, even the 'psycho', has genuinely misheard a word or a phrase delivered against the backdrop of a roaring crowd, a busy street or an airport. And you get nice, polite ones who are 'temps' and simply know sod-all about sport. If you've got 600 words to do on Aston Villa v Arsenal and they want to know if there is an 'h' in Aston, you know you've got big trouble.

Things like that explain how the ATP Trophy appeared in print as 'the 80p trophy', how a football team came to have thirteen players (excluding subs) because the copy-taker thought the initial R, dictated phonetically as 'R for Raymond'—as in Ray Kennedy—was two surnames 'Arthur and Raymond' and how a story about the Polish soccer player Kaz Deyna leaving Manchester City and 'going home to Warsaw because he cannot understand the language', appeared as 'WALSALL'.

Former *Sunday People* sports editor John Maddock recalls an experience when he was reporting a rugby league game for the *Warrington Guardian*. 'There were two players called Major in the Warrington side, so I gave the initials when I dictated the teams to the copy-taker. A while later, the copy-taker rang me back and said he was having trouble with the sports desk over the teams. He said he had a Major W and a Major H and could I give him their surnames!'

I mean to say, rugby league teams are full of Ponsonby-Smythes, Farquharsons and the odd brigadier, aren't they?

Classic misprints include when the Irish soccer team Crusaders appeared as 'Crewe Sailors', when 'chunky Sammy Lee' became 'junkie Sammy Lee' and how the great golfer Max Faulkner was transformed from 'the sweet-swinging star of yesteryear' to 'the street-singing star of yesteryear'. For months after that the embarrassed golfer was subjected to choruses of *Only a Rose* and *Be my Love* in locker rooms around the globe.

Talking of golf ... a certain national newspaper correspondent who was universally hated by the copy takers because
of his massive ego and inherent rudeness, was about to dictate
his report on The Open Championship. It was so close to edition
time he couldn't wait until the presentation ceremony, also about
to start just a few yards away, had taken place. So he grunted a
warning to the copy-taker in his usual condescending manner.
'From time to time during my report you may hear bursts of
applause,' to which the copy-taker replied cynically 'Why, is it
that bloody good?'

Frank McGhee, the *Daily Mirror's* chief football writer
for many years, was covering one of the great European games
at Liverpool in the Shankly era. The story goes that he began
dictating copy something like this: 'Liverpool produced another
glory night at Anfield when they crushed the pride of Italian
football ... '

At that point, the copy-taker, a 'casual' and an Indian
unfamiliar with Liverpool or football, interjected. 'Excuse me,
Mr McGhee but I am stopping you because your grammar is
incorrect.' 'What are you talking about? There's nothing wrong
with my grammar ... just take the copy ... the desk want it NOW,'
snapped Frank.

'I am sorry, Mr McGhee, but I am insisting you are wrong.
You are very fine writer but I am knowing from my school in
Bombay what is gram-mat-ic-ally correct. You can say 'a field'
or 'the field' but you cannot say 'an field'.'

Malcolm Brodie, that doyen of Irish sports writers who
has never forgiven me for taking his raincoat by mistake after
an awards luncheon in London (it was the nearest I came to
getting an award) has reported the ups and downs of Northern
Ireland's footballers for decades. The pinnacle, perhaps, was a
game I also had the good fortune to attend, when the Irish beat
Spain, the host nation, in Valencia in the 1982 World Cup Finals.

An ecstatic MB began his report to the *Belfast Telegraph*,
where he was Sports editor for 42 years, with the salute

'Magnifico, magnifico, magnifico.' Back down the telephone line came the equally excited voice of the copy-taker 'It's okay Malcolm, I heard you the first time.'

Direct-dial calls have minimised one problem reporters used to encounter, particularly when making long-distance reverse-charge calls. You had to give the operator your name and, if he or she didn't quite catch it, spell it out phonetically like wartime fighter pilots and police officers. You know the stuff 'C for Charlie, D for Dog, T for Tango etc.'

R. J. Rutnagur, that distinguished and long-serving cricket correspondent for the *Daily Telegraph*, has a style all his own. The story goes that he put in a call to his office from a Test match in Calcutta and was asked for his name. 'Rutnagur,' he said, slowly and politely. 'Sorry, I didn't quite catch it. Would you mind spelling it for me,' replied the international operator. 'Certainly. R for Rajah, U for Urdu, T for Taj Mahal, N for Nawab of Pataudi, A for Aga Khan, G for Ghandi, U for Urdu and R for Rajasthan ... ' Absolutely superb.

I have phoned copy from some fairly bizarre places but nothing beats Hamburg's 'red light' district on a wet Sunday afternoon. Driving back from a world championship speedway meeting in Denmark, to catch a flight to Heathrow, my travelling companions insisted we while away a few hours in the notorious Rieperbahn. Strangely enough I had no objections but I did have a *Daily Express* deadline to meet.

It was a good story, too ... for speedway. Six-times world champion Ivan Mauger had announced he was quitting the sport he had distinguished for so many years. It was one of those stories that didn't really need writing with speedway regarded as a fringe sport. Seven or eight pars with quotes, ad-lib, no sweat. Unfortunately, I had no free-phone number and you couldn't make collect calls from West Germany.

Short of sufficient coinage to use a pay phone, I was getting a bit desperate when I spotted a phone on a bar as we passed an open door. I dived in, ordered a beer and the barman understood my request to pay for a quick call to London office for them to ring me straight back.

Within seconds the return call came through and I was on to the copy-taker. A girl. I started dictating 'From Dick Julian (one of many pseudonyms I used in those days) dateline Vojens, Denmark, Sunday ... .'

Naively, I suppose, I hadn't realised I was in a bar showing hard-core blue movies, on big screens above my head, to the right and left. Suddenly, I was distracted by the vigorous copulating on screen and, trying to concentrate on filing a few paragraphs, ad lib, became a real problem.

In a situation like that, the most trivial words and phrases suddenly take on a double entendre, e.g. 'Ivan Mauger is pulling out ... he says it is a hard decision ... the man who has done it more times than anyone else ... he has been on top for years ... etc.' The copy-taker sensed something was amiss and when I explained, she was more interested in the movie than Ivan Mauger. She wasn't the only one.

I have had similarly uproariously risqué conversations with gay copy-takers. They used to have one on the *Daily Telegraph* in Manchester, a dead ringer for John Inman's camp character in the TV sit-com Are you being served? He was a real hoot and, let me say first and foremost, a first-class copy-taker. I filed a story about a decathlete whose pole snapped. 'Ooh, the poor luv, how is he going to have a jump now?' Once, without thinking, I said 'Hello, it's Bott of Manchester. I've just got a short piece for you!'

Maybe copy-takers are just unfortunates who are misunderstood but, often, so are correspondents. Take the Irish freelance who liked to hit the bottle so much the copy takers at one national newspaper complained to the news desk that he was always drunk when he came on with a story and, more often than not, it was utter gibberish. So the instruction went out 'Don't take copy from O'Reilly of Dublin (the name has been changed for obvious reasons), unless he is sober.'

There was a bit of a panic on the London news desk this particular night because they had an off-beat story that needed a couple of verses of the old classic Irish song 'McNamara's Band' to embellish it. But nobody could remember more than a line or two of the lyric and even the office library drew a blank.

Then somebody had a flash of inspiration. 'Call O'Reilly, he'll know the words.' They phoned him up, he did know the words of the song and he was sober, so they put him through to the copy-takers and assured him he wouldn't have a problem this time. 'Don't worry, Paddy, they are expecting your call. All we want are the words of the song.'

'Hello, darlings, it's O'Reilly of Dublin here ... I have some ordered copy for you,' he said. 'Okay, Mr O'Reilly, when you're ready'. 'My name is McNamara I'm the leader of the band,' he began. At which point, the copy-taker pulled the plug. 'Nothing changes, he's pissed again!'

Ten

THE EGO HAS LANDED

WE all like to see our name in lights. Nice picture, big by-line. I'm no exception. But I think and hope I would seriously struggle to get into the Premier League when it comes to vanity. And I have to be careful here or I could lose the few friends I have left. It's going to be a case of 'if the cap fits'. You may recall that clever ditty Carly Simon used to sing: 'You're so vain ... you probably think this song is about you.' We'll see.

Fleet Street used to be like the lawns of a stately home, full of strutting peacocks. Northern offices of national newspapers had reporters and production staffs—and a few poseurs—but all the big-name editors, writers and columnists were in London and it was only when you got down there that you found they all thought their editing, their column in their paper, gardening, theatre, television, finance, politics, business, travel, gossip, sport, whatever, was responsible for the circulation. They would hold court in different fashionable wine bars and bistros while their camp followers hung on every self-opinionated word.

The most popular watering holes in the 'street' were heaving with egos as well as bosoms. Vince Wilson, the *Sunday Mirror's* northern sports writer, had his dad down from Seaham Harbour for a Cup Final and the old feller's observation was priceless. 'Everybody speaks but nobody listens,' he said.

A bit like *Hold the Back Page!*

I know a few sports writers and broadcasters, north and south, who are so vain that if a ball, cricket, football, golf, rugby or tennis, landed in their lap in the press box during a match, they would autograph it before throwing it back. The same goes for a few editors and sports editors. You know the type of thing. '*Mirror, Mirror* on the wall, who is the greatest editor/news editor/sports editor/dictator of them all?'

Vanity manifests itself in different ways; in appearance, in demeanour, in power, in arrogance, in print. Much of it is fairly harmless. The designer shades, the Versace suit, the coiffure, the mobile you talk to when it's switched off; the Grecian 2000, the wig, the bracelets, the tan from a bottle. The sports car. The racing driver gloves when you haven't got a sports car.

The golf writer who poses by the practice green at The Open Championship, wearing a designer cap, expensive golf shoes and a monogrammed pullover with a putter dangling over his shoulder is simply rubbing both shoulders with his fantasies. Likewise the soccer writer on tour with club or country who ambles into the foyer of the hotel in a replica kit, the laces trailing from his Reeboks, with that I've-just-been-training-and-its-so-good look.

A certain television presenter used to make it a habit on foreign trips, in his social-climbing days on local radio, to get the hotel to page him in the bar or restaurant even if there was no message or phone call. Nothing original about that. The late Des Hackett and Henry Rose of the *Daily Express* were famous for it.

And I believe the entrepreneur Barry Hearn could teach them all a trick or two ... using a similar ploy. In the days before he became a household name, I'm told he would ask hotels and restaurants to page 'Lord Hearn'. Once 'recognised' you can imagine he had no trouble being waited on hand and foot.

A trio of big-name London soccer writers, who liked to 'Hollywood a bit' and were as inseparable as the Beverley Sisters, were nick-named 'The Morris Men' and often greeted by colleagues shaking imaginary tambourines. Later they incorporated a 'junior' member who was known, affectionately

as 'Morris Minor'. I suppose it was their way of sticking two—
or even three—fingers up to the rest of us when they turned it to
their lucrative advantage by producing books for the Carling
Premiership as Morrismen Productions.

Some writers pack for a week when they are only going
to be away for a couple of nights. On one trip into Europe, a
colleague pointed to another scribe in the hotel foyer. 'Would
you look at him. We've only been here a few hours and that's
his third ensemble!' Who says only women are bitchy?

Can you believe I sat next to a top writer in the press box
at one Wembley Cup Final and he wrote his entire match report
in Italian and dictated it in English—because he found the game
so boring. He did mention it, just in case I hadn't noticed.
Another used to get to Wembley early enough to walk round
the stadium counting his posters on the fences and lamp posts
and sulk if a rival had more than him. The posters should have
read 'Golden Bollocks is here today'.

We all exchange greetings with friends or acquaintances
who wander past the press box just before kick-off time but
very few of us stand up affectedly and shout, in decibels that
challenge the tannoy 'Nice to see you ... you've got a mention
in my new book!' What's the subject ... narcissism?

I was strolling round the cricket ground at Harrogate one
Saturday morning a few summers ago, back in my home town
watching Yorkshire play—legitimately on this occasion because
I was working. The game was in progress and I stopped,
momentarily, to watch the next ball. A public school voice rang
out from the front porch of the groundsman's cottage just behind
me. 'I say, old chap, do you mind moving just a trifle towards
third man because you are obstructing my vision.'

The tones were familiar and I turned to see a well-known
national paper cricket correspondent, sprawling in a deck-chair
wearing his Cambridge University sweater and cap. And, if I
was not mistaken, with a chilled glass of Chardonnay at his
elbow.

Some cricket writers, of the full-time, all-day, from-first-ball-to-stumps variety, tend to have an aloofness few can equal. Whether it comes into the category of arrogance rather than vanity is debatable. Maybe it's a shield against boredom.

Along with the Lord Snootys and 'medallion men' of other sports they just need to be put down, not by a vet but by acid wit.

In my experience, the master of the 'put down' was the late Dick Williamson, of the *Bradford Telegraph and Argus*, who covered soccer and cricket in Yorkshire with a sharp eye, a sharp mind, a sharp pen and the bluntest of tongues. If he saw an ego loose in the press box he treated it like a cockroach.

The vain talk ill of each other but never to their faces. So it often needed someone like Dick, of the gnarled features and rakish trilby, to deliver a suitable riposte. A legend among cricket writers and broadcasters was tiresomely arrogant at times and one day, when Yorkshire were playing on Dick's home patch, Bradford Park Avenue, spent most of the afternoon session whingeing about one thing or another.

At one point he wailed 'This is a calamity. I have broken a tooth and I'm due on air again in five minutes.' The uncomfortable silence was pierced when old Dick looked up from his seat in the corner and rasped 'Come back and tell us when you've broken your bleedin' neck!'

The best put-down I ever heard was when a distinguished sports writer arrived late in the press box for a cricket match and complained, at some length, about being 'mugged' on the way to the ground. He was not the most popular member of the cricket-writing fraternity and there was hardly a groundswell of sympathy for him as he whinged on about racism and how he had only been a victim of the assault because of his colour. It was a tricky one. Suddenly, a comment triggered an explosion of laughter. Another writer of similar colour and origin delivered the immortal line: 'You were not mugged because you are black, you were mugged because you are a c***!'

Fame cultivates vanity among some sportsmen and women. They swan around in fancy cars and suits and complain if the club only provides them with one gardener. Others are outrageously tongue in cheek. Big Ron Atkinson, one of my favourite managers, used to chide the press for creating a 'Champagne Charlie' image for him when he maintained he never wore gold bracelets and preferred 'a cup of rosy'. Yet I can't believe any other football manager in history has conducted his Friday morning press conference lying on a sunbed in his office. Ron argues the sunbed was only there temporarily and that he was pushed for time—but no jury is going to accept that.

The fact is, m'lud, I was one of the Manchester-based soccer writers sat round this enormous sunbed while Ron took off his Manchester United towelling robe, put on a pair of goggles, and pulled the lid down like Count Dracula. We took notes from the disembodied voice, mesmerised by the ultra-violet glow around the edges of the 'coffin'.

Eventually, when Ron emerged, the inimitable John Bean of the *Daily Express* cracked 'It's not worked Ron, you're still brown!'

A story I think best illustrates the vanity of some sports stars concerns the England soccer international striker who picked up a girl in a night club and whisked her off to his hotel room. As they lay naked in the bed, the besotted girl eager for action, the player took her hand and placed it on his right leg. 'Feel this leg? It's scored 16 goals this season,' he bragged. Then he placed her hand on his left leg. 'Feel this leg, it's scored 12 goals this season.' Then he placed her hand on his forehead and gushed 'Feel my head ... it's scored ten goals including four for England.'

In frustration, the girl grabbed the player's hand and placed it between her legs. 'Yes, but have you ever felt one of these before?' The player, without a second thought, replied 'Yes ... when I missed a penalty against City!'

Eleven

THE IRISH ARE WONDERFUL

OF all the countries I have been fortunate enough to visit, I love Ireland the best. North and south the people are warm and hospitable, the salmon and the Guinness is magnificent and I envy their laid-back attitude to life and their extraordinary logic. I used to hate it. It was too laid back, too slow and their logic too bizarre.

Only a few years ago I telephoned the Football Association of Ireland offices in Dublin from the *Sunday Express* in Manchester. It was a Saturday morning and I needed to check out a story with the then general secretary. Eventually, I got through and asked to speak to him. 'There's no one here today!'

Okay, I could see the logic in that. So I rang his home number. Whoever answered said 'I'm sorry but he's out. Have you tried his office?' 'Yes, but he's not there either.' 'Ah, that'll be because he doesn't go in on a Saturday!' I was still reeling from that one when the voice suggested, very politely 'If you press button B you may get your money back!'

Ireland is the only country in the world where I have ever seen a cross-roads sign at a T junction. It was five miles to Navan—through the middle of a grocer's shop.

My first wife was from Boyle, in County Roscommon, and my sister-in-law and her family now live in beautiful County Mayo. It was in the west, nearly forty years ago, that I had my first taste of the Irish sporting scene, as a spectator at minor hurling and gaelic football games. Then, in the late Sixties, when I had just started writing for the *Sunday Express* in a free-lance capacity. Sport was such a serious business in England. In

Ireland, in those days, some of it seemed less so. I was on a working holiday, looking for a few features and stories for the Irish edition. Too much, they told me, focused on Dublin.

So I picked up the weekly paper *The Roscommon Herald* and read a couple of paragraphs about an athletics event that was taking place nearby the following day—a 50 kilometre road walk that was being used as an official trial for the forthcoming Olympic Games. Apparently, two Irish walkers, who had been at colleges in the USA, were coming over to try to get inside the qualifying time.

It sounded newsworthy enough to me so I went along. The event co-incided with the local carnival at Lough Arrow and the start and finish point was outside the marquee where copious quantities of Guinness were being supped all day and most of the night.

Sure enough the two college boys turned up, fit and smart and ready to go, and a few others would have passed for athletes in most places. But as for the rest. What a motley crew. Some of them didn't look capable of walking as far as the next beer tent. But someone shouted 'Good luck, lads,' blew a whistle and off they went.

What threw me completely was an incident some ten minutes later. A car pulled up outside the marquee, with a screech of its brakes, and a red-faced youth got out. 'Have I missed the start, Seamus?' he enquired, with a degree of urgency. 'By about ten minutes, Michael,' replied the fellow who had started the race. 'But you'll catch them if you RUN!' And with that, the youth peeled off his shirt and trousers, pinned a number to his vest and set off down the road like a whippet. The 50 kilometre WALK, the official Olympic trial, was off and running.

The two college boys came home, first and second and inside the qualifying time, and saw nothing strange or remotely illegal about anything the rest of the field had got up to. They could have rowed across the lake for all they cared, as long as it didn't affect the result. The officials didn't bat an eye-lid either. They were more interested in 'Big Tom and the Mainliners' and whether the supply of Guinness would run dry. I should have seen the warning signs.

My next target was the Connaught Athletics Championships in Athlone, that beautiful market town on the Shannon in Westmeath, right in the centre of the country. Tom somebody or other, a 33 year old farmer from Galway, was bidding for his eighth or ninth consecutive championship in the mile and there were a few young bucks looking for Olympic places. This sounded like serious stuff.

I headed for Athlone the following Sunday and looked for something resembling an athletics stadium. Not a chance. The Connaught Championships took place five miles out of town in a hay field, on an undulating surface as precarious as a minefield. I watched the racing and stumbling and the farmer from Galway duly won the mile again with a thundering finish. The time? Four minutes, five seconds. I couldn't believe it. And I became increasingly suspicious when the championship record was smashed out of sight in almost every track event.

I asked the farmer if he was surprised he had run the mile 15 seconds faster than ever before. A little, he said, but he had been training hard.

With no disrespect to the track officials, most of them had been imbibing and seemed oblivious to the need to press the button on their watches when races started or finished. I fancied the best thing was to get the home phone number of the meeting organiser and then wait to see what the *Irish Independent* and the *Irish Times* made of it all the next day. I expected 'Records blitzed in Athlone' at the very least.

I walked into Boyle to buy the morning papers and found the Connaught Championships blithely dismissed in a couple of paragraphs. Then I looked at the results and times. The winners were the same but the times were all different--all SLOWER! I thought the Guinness or the Jamesons had got to me. It couldn't have been the sun. It hardly ever shone in Boyle when I was there.

I phoned the meeting organiser for an explanation and within minutes the *Sunday Express* had a purler of an exclusive. It seems somebody had queried the high number of track records in relation to the long grass and bumpy track and decided to measure it again. It was found to be well short of the statutory 440 yards and also short where they held the sprints. Only then did the 'groundsman' confess he had paced out the track because his measuring equipment had broken down.

The logic of the officials, armed with this information an hour or so after the conclusion of the championships, was to amend the winning times by a few seconds or fractions of seconds here and there before releasing the results to the press. They had to be joking. But they weren't. My sports editor thought 'the great Irish cock-up' was a fantastic story and told me to file it and then enjoy the rest of my holiday. That wasn't the end of it because it never appeared in print.

Apparently, someone in Dublin or London went to the Irish Athletics Association for the official view and they white-washed the whole thing, denied all the stuff about pacing out the track and changing the times. The message seemed to be that it wasn't unusual so why make a fuss about it. It took me years to get over that one.

I am sure Irish sport, at the top level, has always been run far more professionally. Indeed, I have had the privilege of interviewing some of the country's sporting legends from way back, the double Olympic hammer gold medallist Doctor Patrick O'Callaghan, the 1,500 metres Olympian Ronnie Delaney and the former Walker Cup star Joe Carr.

Doctor Pat was an amazing athlete way back in the 20's and 30's. I did my homework on him, from the cuttings library, before I flew over to Dublin and drove down the east coast to meet him at his home in Tramore. I had heard he was a great story-teller with a flamboyant personality, even in his seventies.

I sat there in his lounge and, for an hour, struggled to get a decent sentence out of him. Then the penny dropped. 'Do you fancy a pint?' I queried. 'Surely we'd be better off doing this over a glass of something.' 'Now you're TALKING,' he said, rising from his chair like the phoenix from the ashes.

We walked down the street to his local tavern, drank the night away and, between the songs and the pints, he filled my notebook with wonderful stories and anecdotes. It taught me a lesson ... never come between an Irishman and his drink.

I was in Spain in 1982 with Northern Ireland in the World Cup Finals, Germany in 1988 with the Republic of Ireland for the European Football Championships and many a time at Windsor Park, Belfast, or Lansdowne Road, Dublin.

You are always more aware of the troubles, that have brought so much grief and suffering to catholics and protestants alike, when you are north of the border. When England went back to play in Belfast in 1983, after a four-year gap, the English press were taken for a magnificent lunch in an equally magnificent country pub/restaurant. The view of the surrounding hills and forests from the main entrance door was so enchanting, you wondered how anything could disturb the peace.

It was only when we were getting back on our bus that I realised you couldn't see the entrance door from outside because it was one-way glass. I asked why, very naively, and was told 'So a sniper couldn't pick you off if you were standing in the doorway.' A chilling thought.

On a later visit to Belfast, I stayed with the Northern Ireland team in the superb Culloden Hotel in the Hollywood district to the north east of the city. Our coach had to pass through the hotel's elaborate security checkpoint, walls and gates topped with barbed wire and a check-in post like a sentry box. It was a beautiful morning and I went for a stroll in the hotel grounds, through the extensive gardens and down to the tennis courts and the Alpine steak house. There I found an open gate leading to a country lane. I walked, without a care, for another five or ten minutes, until I found myself on another road and right OUTSIDE the main entrance again. So much for security, I thought.

I think that was the night the press box at Windsor Park was evacuated soon after the full-time whistle because the police received a warning that mortars were trained on the stadium. Even Billy Bingham, the Northern Ireland manager, left at the gallop.

During the ceasefire, in 1994, I covered the Northern Ireland-Republic of Ireland European Championships game in Belfast, when the Republic won 4-0. As a Sunday paper man, I had a seat in the 'overflow' because the glass-fronted press box was full. No problem. Nice to sit in the crowd and savour the atmosphere. I had been assured 'There'll be no trouble tonight because they haven't sold any tickets to the Republic and the ceasefire is in force anyway.'

But you know how it is, some fans can always get tickets and they can't help their spontaneous reactions. So when the first Republic goal went in, a devotee of Jack Charlton's 'Boys in Green' could not contain himself. He was up hollering and punching the air like a good 'un. Immediately, an Ulsterman to my left, leapt to his feet, puce with rage and roared 'Stick your semtex up your arse, you Fenian bastard!' Funny, you don't hear too much of that at Old Trafford or Highbury.

The real humour comes from the capacity the Irish have to laugh at themselves. Long before they produced a swimmer, in Michelle Smith, who struck gold three times in the Atlanta Olympics, they openly acknowledged their incompetence in the water. Who can forget this immortal line from one of their most distinguished sports writers 'The good news about the Irish swimming team at the Olympic pool this morning was that nobody drowned'.

I believe the Irish golfer Eamon D'Arcy was once asked at a press conference 'What was your best placing on the

European tour?' 'Fifth,' he replied. Another journalist queried 'Was that the Swedish Open?' 'No,' said D'Arcy, 'I was fourth in that!'

I have always enjoyed the company of Irish sports writers and, since I left the *Sunday Express* in September 1996, have had the opportunity to cover English football for Dublin's fast-growing all-sports Sunday supplement *The Title*. I was invited to be their guest at the Irish soccer writers dinner in May 1997 when they honoured, among others, an old pal of mine.

Alfie Hale, one of the legends of Irish soccer who I first knew when he played in England for Aston Villa and Doncaster Rovers, was back in Waterford in the late 60's and in August 1970 his team played a pre-season friendly against Blackpool, who had just been promoted to the First Division. I drove down from Boyle to cover it for the *Sunday Express*. Waterford were the League of Ireland champions and Blackpool thrashed them 9-0. I asked Alfie for his assessment of their chances in the First Division. 'They'll have to play a hell of a lot better than that or they'll go straight back down,' he said. And he was proved right because they did but it just seemed such a daft thing to say at the time.

Around that period Finn Harps joined the League of Ireland and I travelled north from Boyle to Ballybofey, in County Donegal, in the hope of talking to their chairman and guru Fran Fields, sadly no longer with us. When I found him he gave me a great story—and a pig! He had a bacon-curing plant in his back garden and it was a present for showing an interest in his club. I took it back to Boyle and we shared it out amongst my mother in law's neighbours.

It was the start of a good friendship which proved very fruitful for me later, particularly when Fran became president of the FAI. I went over to Donegal when Everton played Finn Harps in the UEFA Cup in September 1978 and did a feature for the *Sunday Express* on their evergreen goalkeeper Eddie Mahon.

He was 36 years old, a wholesale wine merchant and bottler in Derry and had been playing senior football for 17 years. He had good contacts in America and told me he was offered a job in New York, with an office in Park Avenue, a private plane and a five-year contract worth £360,000. He turned it down. Why? 'I'd miss my football too much.' I asked him how much longer he planned to carry on. 'Oh, I'll pack it in next season because I'm getting too many injuries!' That is Irish logic.

There must have been a streak of Irish in Rotherham United's Yorkshire-born goalkeeper Gordon Morritt, who told his manager he couldn't play in a 4-3-3 formation because he'd only just got used to 4-4-2.

Eddie Mahon did concede that he wasn't too fond of flying and on his regular business trips to England went by car, using the ferry from Larne to Stranraer. On one such trip, the police found his car on the hard shoulder of the M6 near Carlisle and spotted a man in a track suit, jogging in a field. It was Eddie. 'They wanted to know what the hell I was doing. So I put on my best Paddy accent and said I was an Irish footballer and that was the time of day I normally trained with the lads in Derry and I didn't want to miss a session! They let me go.'

My trip to Donegal that year was memorable for the most astonishing example of Irish logic I have come across. Fran Fields, ever generous and hospitable, had told Everton he would meet their players and officials at Dublin Airport and give their team coach an escort to Donegal, cutting across the corner of Ulster to save them the long drive west to Sligo and up the north west coast. After all, it could be a bit precarious going through Ulster unprotected.

Fran also invited me to travel in his car, with the former Everton and Irish international Peter Farrell, to 'mark my card' on the Finn Harps team (which was how I came to interview Eddie Mahon). So, once we landed in Dublin, I took the front passenger seat in Fran's car with Peter now in the back. Can you believe that somehow we managed to lose the Everton coach before we had left the perimeters of the airport and after doubling back a few times, Fran decided to try to catch up en route. We never saw the coach again until we stopped for tea in Enniskillen two hours later.

Along the way, we crossed the border into Ulster and had been driving through Fermanagh for about half an hour when there was a crack and the sound of splintering glass. The rear window had gone. 'What the hell was that?' asked Peter, hitting the floor. If it wasn't a gun shot, it sounded like one. 'Just a stone kicked up by a passing car,' said Fran, unconvincingly. I say that because stones don't normally break rear windows unless vehicles are stationary and Fran went through the next two villages at about eighty miles an hour.

Not much was said until we hit a nice stretch of open country and cruised for a few miles. We had just passed a road junction when an RUC patrol car spotted us and signalled for us to stop. They had seen the shattered window AND the southern Irish registration plates. Two members of the RUC, guns at the ready, approached our car.

The conversation went something like this:

POLICEMAN: 'Would you be giving me your name, sir?'

FRAN: 'Fran Fields, chairman of Finn Harps Football Club, Ballybofey, County Donegal.'

POLICEMAN: 'Have you any means of identification, sir?'

FRAN: (rummaging in his pockets and the glove compartment) 'Not really but the man with me is a football reporter from England and this is my good friend Peter Farrell. If you're on about the window, a stone hit it.'

POLICEMAN: (Highly suspicious) 'Would you be after telling me what you are doing in this area, with southern plates on, and where you are heading?'

FRAN: 'Sure, we're escorting the Everton Football Club coach to Donegal for a UEFA Cup game.'

The two policemen looked back down the deserted country road where you could see for a good mile and the only sound came from the twittering of birds. The senior officer spoke again and touched his cap 'Right then, sir, that's fine. Have a good journey.' Now that's Irish logic.

Wonderful country, wonderful people and a lot smarter than you think, as a Texan farmer discovered in conversation with an Irish farmer over a few snorts of Jamesons somewhere in Tipperary.

'How big is your farm?' asked the Texan. 'It stretches as far as the eye can see', said the Irishman. 'That's nothing,' bragged the American. 'I can get in my car at six in the morning and at midnight I'm still on my own land.' 'Funny,' said the Irishman, dryly 'I used to have a car like that.'

Twelve

MANAGERS

IT is a sad state of affairs when a job consumes you to the extent that you think of nothing else, not even your family. It happens in many walks of life, including journalism, and it certainly happens to some football managers. I interviewed one who was having a rough time and his predicament was aggravated by family problems.

I tried to be sympathetic. 'You've had a lot of problems at home.' He looked at me, accusingly, and said 'That's a bit out of order. We've only lost three and should have won at least four of the five we've drawn.'

The turnover in football managers, at all levels, is staggeringly high, the pressure more intense than it has ever been. Now the intrusive eye of television captures all the agony and ecstasy in close-up you can practically watch the ageing process at work. The camera homes in on the bench or dug-out to focus on every anguished twitch and grimace, every explosion of joy or relief, every glance at the watch. Some disguise their emotions better than others but do you really think Ruud Gullit is so laid back he doesn't give a damn? Or that Bryan Robson's inscrutable features during a match are a sign of indifference?

Managers don't like talking about pressure but it's there from the moment they wake up in the morning until the moment they fall asleep at night; if they get any. And when people like Kenny Dalglish and Kevin Keegan, two of the most successful, most experienced men in the game, walk away from top jobs, you know its getting tougher at all levels. And it has never been easy. Joe Mercer put it into perspective a couple of decades ago when he said 'People either want your hand or your head in this business.'

The pressure starts in your own dressing-room, trying to keep all your players reasonably happy. Another late and lamented manager, the great Jock Stein, had a wonderful philosophy. 'You have to keep the six players who hate you away from the five who haven't yet made up their minds.' That's more like it.

What a manager needs above all else is a sense of humour; an escape valve. Dario Gradi, who was appointed manager of Crewe in June 1983 and is now the longest-surviving one-club manager in the four divisions, told me a lovely story when I called in at Gresty Road. 'I remember coming here as manager of Wimbledon. It was an awful place, with no room to move about in the dressing rooms and with a corrugated iron fence that was falling down. I said to the players "You'd better listen to what I tell you and do as you're told or you might end up here". Instead of them, it was me.'

No manager I have ever known was more steeped in football or his work than Bill Shankly. Wasn't it Shanks who coined the phrase that football was more important than life or death? Yet he had a way with the one-liners long before he turned Liverpool Football Club into an institution. He was the manager of Grimsby Town before floodlights and they were hanging on to a 1-0 lead as the light faded. The referee came across to the dug-out, summoned the two managers and said 'I'm going to have to call it off ... it's too dark.' Shanks argued: 'The light's fine.' 'But I can't see,' protested the referee. Shanks pointed up through the murk at the moon. 'What's that then, referee?' 'It's the moon, of course.' 'Well how far do you want to see?'

Shankly stories are part of football folklore, far beyond Merseyside. My favourite is one Bob Paisley used to relate about an incident when Bill was emptying his desk just after his shock decision to retire, in the summer of 1974. The phone rang and Bob answered. 'It's for you, Bill. Adidas. They want to make you a golden boot to mark your retirement.' 'Real gold?' asked Shanks. 'I think so.' 'Then tell them "yes" and that I take size thirteen!'

He was an intimidating man by nature. I went to his home in Liverpool—remarkably enough, next door to Everton's training ground—to do an interview and he invited me into his lounge. Then he signalled for me to sit down on the settee while he pulled up a dining room chair, turned it round, and sat leaning on the back of it, towering above me. 'Right, Richard, what do you want to ask me?'

It was the type of intimidatory tactic several managers have used to deal with players, particularly those looking for a pay rise. Allan Clarke told me he used the same ploy when he became manager of Leeds United.

All Shankly's players worshipped him and tell great stories of how he motivated them and mentally demolished the opposition. He demolished the press, too, if they touched a nerve. I was at a game Liverpool played against Sheffield United at Anfield when a young Tony Currie was in bewitching form for the visitors and the result went against Shankly's Reds. Questions had to be couched in sympathetic terms on days like that, unless you wanted a flea in your ear.

After a few minutes of gentle probing, a fresh-faced young reporter from Sheffield asked Shanks if he had been impressed with Currie's performance. 'Aye, he did alright,' rasped Bill. The reporter persisted, looking for a local angle, but pushed his luck too far. Knowing Shanks had always been a great admirer of Tom Finney, he dared to suggest Currie might be worthy of comparison with the former Preston and England legend. Hardened hacks recoiled in horror and waited for the explosion. Shanks simply rubbed a finger over his chin, stared hard at the floor and, without shifting his gaze, answered 'Aye, you could be right, son.' Then, after a suitable pause, he added 'But what you have to remember is that Tony Currie is 23 and Tom Finney is nearly 53!'

The amazing Shanks was out-punchlined once, on Liverpool's first-ever adventure into European competition. The year was 1964, the month August, and Liverpool set out to visit the champions of Iceland, KR Reykjavik. A roundabout route was to take them from Liverpool's Speke Airport, via London and Glasgow, to the Icelandic capital.

But as my good pal Norman Wynne, then with the *Sunday People*, recalls: 'We had a fair bit of time to kill in Scotland because the flight to Reykjavik didn't take off until midnight. So Shanks decided to take us all to Butlin's Holiday Camp in Ayr. When the coach rolled up at the front entrance, Shanks said to us "Leave this to me, boys, and I'll get us in for nothing." Then he leaned out of the door and said to the gateman "Bill Shankly and Liverpool Football club ... en route to Iceland for a European Cup game".' The gate man replied, dryly 'Do you no think you've maybe taken the wrong turning?'

Staying with Liverpool, for a moment, Bob Paisley could deliver a few punch-lines. When he signed the versatile Israeli international Avi Cohen from Macabbi Tel Aviv he was warned 'If he's a Muslim he won't be able to play on Saturdays.' Bob cracked 'We've got a few like that already.' And when he was left to carry the can for Terry McDermott, who failed to turn up at a London hotel to receive his Footballer of the Year award from the soccer writers, in 1980, he snapped 'If this is one of his famous blind-side runs, it will be the last one he makes for Liverpool.'

Kenny Dalglish, outstanding as both a player and a manager, has always represented a challenge to the media. He can see a headline coming a mile away and puts up the barricades. Sometimes the answers smack of sarcasm. 'How close was Beardsley to playing today?' 'Well, he was in the dressing room and you canna get much closer than that.' Generally, he treats banal questions with the contempt they deserve but football is full of banalities and clichés. Managers excel at them. 'We take one game at a time ... we got what we deserved—nothing ... we did enough to win ... etc.'

Dalglish has always been modest to a fault, another facet of his personality that makes it so difficult to get him talking on a day-to-day basis. And he ducks most requests for one-on-one interviews.

There is a tale that, during the 1988-89 season when he was manager of Liverpool, he met his match in a down-to-earth Yorkshire sports writer from the *Halifax Evening Courier*. Halifax Town had a young striker called Terry McPhillips, a lad who had been released by the Anfield club where he had been a trainee.

McPhillips was having an outstanding season, scoring goals for fun and attracting the interest of a number of big clubs. *The Courier* thought it would be a good angle to get a quote or two from Dalglish and their reporter telephoned Anfield several times for several days in an attempt to contact the Liverpool manager, displaying admirable persistence.

At last, the reporter got through, more by luck than judgement, and said 'Hello Kenny, it's the *Halifax Evening Courier* ... we'd like a few quotes from you about Terry McPhillips?' 'Terry McWho?' came the rhetorical reply. 'Thank you very much Kenny, that will do nicely,' said the *Courier* man and put down the phone. That night, his newspaper splashed the back page with the headline 'Terry McWho?' and a lead story that the Liverpool manager had never heard of the young striker he had shown the door. Full marks for their cheek.

Talking of Halifax ... when that big-hearted northern lad John McGrath was manager at The Shay a few years later, and the club was lurching from one financial crisis to another, he could always bring a bit of sunshine to the darkest day. He cracked 'I'm ready to listen to offers for all my players and even Benny, the club cat. He's pissed off because there's no mice to catch. They've all died of starvation'.

And talking of Kenny Dalglish, again, he maintains that he is wary of the press because his words and remarks have been 'twisted' or taken out of context too often in the past. Not always by the writers, he concedes. Maybe he is not given credit often enough for a sense of humour as dry as the desert, although it did seem to go AWOL when Dalglish's current club, Newcastle, played non-league Stevenage in the F.A. Cup.

During his successful reign as Liverpool's manager, he banned the *Daily Star* although he respected their Merseyside reporter Matt D'Arcy. It is common for disagreements with the media to be comparatively short-lived so, after a week or two, D'Arcy called at the training ground and asked Dalglish 'Am I still banned, Kenny?' 'Aye', said the Scot. 'Is it a life ban?' questioned D'Arcy. 'That depends how long you've got to live, Matt.'

Across Merseyside, a sprawling community of would be comics, a succession of Everton managers have come and gone, some the butt of ridicule, some well capable of holding their own. Howard Kendall, who brought even more success to Goodison Park as a manager than his old mentor Harry Catterick, is back for a third spell in charge. He recalls going to a sports forum in Liverpool soon after beginning his first spell as manager. 'Having been at Everton as a player, I know, as a manager, I will live or die by my results', he told the audience. Back came the instant riposte 'You've got half an hour to live'.

The bubbly Kendall took his players to a local restaurant and, naturally, the waitress took his order first. 'I'll have a fillet steak,' said Howard. 'And what about the vegetables, sir?' 'Oh, they'll have the same.'

Kendall had succeeded Gordon Lee, an honest-as-the-day-is-long Black Country character, who occasionally seemed bewildered by the sheer size of the club and its expectations although he did take Everton to the League Cup Final in his first season in charge and then into Europe twice. On a scouting mission to London, Gordon got off the train at Euston with another member of his backroom staff and was surprised to see club secretary Jim Greenwood and his wife walking down the platform ahead of them. 'What's Jim doing here?' asked

Gordon. 'I think he's going to watch Evita,' was the matter-of-fact reply. 'Evita? Who the hell does he play for?'

Brian Clough's many outstanding qualities as a manager included the art of the 'put-down', a few choice words aimed at keeping a runaway ego in check. One of his players was displaying signs of arrogance so 'Cloughie' rounded on him after a training session. 'Heh, young man, who won two caps for England on the same day?' The puzzled player shook his head. 'Two caps on one day? Don't know, boss.' 'You did, son—your first and your last!'

Peter Withe told me that he asked 'Cloughie' if he could keep the match ball after scoring four goals in a game for Forest. 'When you learn how to play, I'll buy you one,' snapped his manager. Withe, who scored the goal that won the European Cup for Aston Villa in 1982, tells that story against himself and never fails to add that 'Cloughie' not only let him keep the ball but personally went into the opposing dressing room to get it autographed.

Jack Charlton puzzled me when I was trying to interview him while he was overseeing a training session in his time as manager of Sheffield Wednesday.

The players were practising routines on the Hillsborough pitch when Jack motioned me to join him in the home dug-out and started answering my questions. Suddenly, he stood up and said 'We'd better move.' 'Why?' I asked him. 'Because I've just farted!'

I drove up to Carlisle in the early Seventies to speak to a grey-haired Geordie grandfather called Dick Young, who had just become the oldest manager in the Football League at 57, after nineteen years on the coaching staff at Brunton Park. His hobby was training homing pigeons. 'Much easier than dealing with footballers,' he told me. 'If they let you down you just wring their necks.'

The Carlisle connection reminds me of the Aldershot manager who was at his wits end over his club's diabolical away form and had tried just about everything, bullying, coaxing, cajoling. As the team coach set off on the long drive up to Carlisle, he came up with one last desperate measure. He told his players 'You're going to listen to a Max Bygraves tape all the way to Carlisle, whether you like it or not. And, if you don't get a bloody win, you can listen to him all the way back.' They won!

When the former Liverpool and England full back Phil Neal was manager at Bolton he was the constant butt of one particularly critical fan whose voice used to ring out several times a game and was clearly audible in the press box. Stuff like 'Neal ... get that left back off, he's bloody useless' ... 'Get the sub on Neal, this lot couldn't score in a brothel' ... 'Resign, Neal'. One season, the manager was obliged to take a mid-season break for health reasons and was sent abroad by the club. When he returned, his first game back in charge had only been under way a few minutes when, during a lull in play, that same old piercing voice rang out. 'Heh, Neal, I never got mi postcard!'

The late Harry Haslam, who I interviewed when he was manager of Sheffield United, had his own way of dealing with troublesome fans. He told me that when he was a little-known manager in non-league football, his team played an away game at Bedford. He was so sick of the abuse coming his way from behind one goal, he put on a coat and cap during the interval and went and stood in the crowd until he identified the culprit. He smacked him one, did a 'runner' and went back to the dug-out.

Peter Madden, stalwart captain and centre half at Rotherham in the 60's, when they reached the League Cup Final and were knocking on the door of the First Division, is the landlord of my local, Tophams Tavern, in the village of Smithy Bridge near Rochdale. He was a Coldstream Guard in his youth, as hard as a miner's toe-cap, and when he was manager of Darlington a rival manager threatened to give him a good hiding for calling him 'a mad Irishman'. Peter told me 'He called me out of the boardroom and said we would settle it outside. One punch did it. He was on his knees, struggling to get up when a wad of notes fell out of his pocket. I picked it up and thought to myself "Oh good, my first pro fight".'

Not a man to trifle with, big Pete. In his playing days with Rotherham he was sent off after a clash with the Bristol Rovers centre forward Alfie Biggs. Peter retaliated after Biggs grabbed him in the 'lunch box'. He was so angry he got Biggs in a head-lock and dragged him off with him. 'The ref sent us both off but if he hadn't, Biggs was going anyway because I wouldn't let go of him!'

Tommy Docherty and Ron Atkinson have both managed a few top clubs in their time, including Manchester United, and always been good for a laugh with the media. I've quoted Ron elsewhere but another gem that comes to mind was at the usual Friday press conference when he revealed one of his defenders, John Gidman, had suffered a serious leg injury in training the previous day. 'Is he in plaster?' asked one of the scribes. 'No, he's in Marbella,' said Ron.

When he bumped into Cyrille Regis, the striker who had been with him at West Brom, he said 'What's all this crap about you being a born-again Christian and finding God? You worked with him for four years at the Albion.'

Big Ron could be just as sharp with his own kind. Rival manager Ron Saunders had a dig at the Old Trafford boss when Ron was giving his after-match press conference. 'Giving the boys the usual load of old rubbish, Ron?' 'Yes, Ron, just telling them what a good manager you are!'

John Bond was at Manchester City when Big Ron was at Old Trafford and they were lively rivals and both media-conscious. I remember going to 'Bondy's' house in Cheshire one Saturday in the summer of '81, not long after City had lost to Spurs at Wembley. It was a 'dead diary' day for the 'Sundays', no Test match, no Wimbledon, no big golf tournament and I was scratching around for a football story to lead the back page.

A couple of the other 'Sunday' lads had the same idea because they gave me a call on the Saturday lunch-time. We decided to give 'Bondy' a ring, told him the 'problem' and he invited us round for a cuppa. 'See what I can do for you boys,' he said, promisingly. When we got there, we lobbed a few ideas and questions at him but none of them sparked anything and he didn't really have a tale for us.

Suddenly, he picked up the phone, dialled a number and the conversation went something like this 'Andy? It's John Bond. Look, have you made your mind up where you're going yet? No. Right. Would you consider coming to Man City? Okay, give it some thought and we'll get a bid in next week. See yer.'

He put the phone down, turned to us and said 'Okay lads, that do yer? Man City want Andy Gray. No quotes and there wasn't any phone call ... was there? ... but we'll be making an official approach on Monday morning.' Job done. Smashing— even if Gray did end up going to Everton instead.

Tommy Docherty is another very good pal of the media although he likes a 'dig' at us every now and again. Doc is in great demand on the after-dinner circuit and I've had the pleasure of supporting him on a few occasions. He got a cheap laugh at my expense with one of his favourite put-downs: 'I've always believed there was a place for the press but they haven't dug it yet.' I replied 'And I've always had a lot of time for The Doc and if he hadn't had such a good lawyer, he'd be serving it!'

He takes the Mickey out of himself for having had 'more clubs than Jack Nicklaus' and for getting clubs relegated. He took Manchester United into the Second Division but, let's be fair, he brought them back up with one of the most exciting young sides in their history and the fans loved him. But that's not always been the way in his chequered career and after being attacked as he was boarding a train, he had to live with the headline 'The Day the Fan hit the Shit'.

Down the years The Doc has given me some cracking interviews, always laced with anecdotes. Only The Doc could address an audience after his perjury trial saying 'I am donating my entire fee to charity but then you know what a bloody liar I am.' I hasten to add that Tommy was cleared by a jury at the Old Bailey on two counts of perjury and that the verdicts were unanimous.

One of the pieces I did with him, for the *Sunday Express*, was just after he was appointed manager of Preston. The Doc joked 'I was invited for a game of bowls with the Chief Constable of Lancashire. I told him I thought it was a hell of a way to take finger-prints!'

Managers admit the one thing they can be sure of is the sack. There is the old chestnut about the new manager who saw his name written on the door of his office in chalk and said 'That didn't bother me as much as the wet sponge hanging on a nail beside it'. Yet whenever a job becomes vacant, the applications pour in.

Take the England job, for instance. Now you would expect a deluge of applications for that post, from experienced managers and coaches throughout the world. Inevitably, the Football Association's chief executive Graham Kelly, finds himself dealing with a fair proportion of tongue-in-cheek and crackpot applications as well. Fortunately, he can see the funny side.

When the FA were looking for a successor to Graham Taylor, I went to the FA's headquarters at Lancaster Gate to find out just who wanted the job. The applicants for the £150,000-a-year post included a boy scout, an ex-miner, a Subbuteo star and the manager of Mixed Veg FC.

'Many of the applications we receive are from people who seriously believe they could be England's next manager but the majority are tongue-in-cheek, spoof letters along the lines of the Henry Root books. I suppose I could put them all in a book myself and call it 'Root One',' said Kelly.

One applicant, a Londoner, enclosed a holiday snap of himself singing *Agadoo* in Majorca, to illustrate he was comfortable in front of the cameras. Another said he could do 'headless chicken' impersonations, which made him an ideal candidate, and a third said 'as the manager of Mixed Veg FC, I am the ideal man to take over from a turnip'. The Subbuteo player wanted to bring in Kenny Dalglish in charge of 'media relations'.

Whatever the cynics and crackpots think, it's no joke being a football manager but laughter is a great escape valve from the pressures. It may not make them better managers but it should help them live a little longer. And that goes for all of us.

Thirteen

PLAYERS

SPORT wouldn't exist without them, would it? Winners and losers all. Male, female and gender benders. Supreme athletes, honest artisans, posers, cheats, druggies and dreamers from up and down the ability and morality scale.

I have seen club golfers with expensive designer gear and a bag full of the best woods and irons money can buy and they can hardly get beyond the ladies tee. Conversely, I have seen a ten year old with a couple of old hickory-shafted clubs strike the ball so sweetly and so far I've wanted to crawl away into the long grass and die.

As it is, I hold the dubious record of having taken 17 shots on a par three at Bradford Golf Club; a seven iron off the tee, two putts and 14 to get out of a greenside bunker deep enough to bury a Sherman tank. It's the same with football and cricket. Natural talent is one of God's greatest gifts. For the rest of us it's just down to bloody hard work or finding a way to cut the corners. And cheating comes at a price—ask anyone who has been caught using drugs.

The truly gifted are those who excel at more than one sport, like my schoolboy hero Denis Compton. As a kid I sat glued to steam radio listening to him help Arsenal to a 2-0 FA Cup Final win over Liverpool in 1950 and score some majestic 'tons' for Middlesex and England. I think it was his former county colleague Peter Parfitt who told me that when you could bat like 'Compo' you could get runs with a chair leg.

I had the privilege of meeting and working with Denis when he was the cricket correspondent of the *Sunday Express* and he took me on a tour of the Long Room on my first, long overdue visit to Lord's a few years ago. What a gentleman. Absolutely charming. And while he needed a 'ghost writer' for his match reports in later years and often nipped up to the members' bar to share a glass or two with his pals, he always spotted something in the play or the wicket that only came from years of having performed at the very top.

We were in the press box at Old Trafford for a Test against Australia when a succession of fairly mediocre England batsmen came out to face a hostile attack wearing a variety of crash helmets and visors. 'Don't recall you wearing anything on your head against Lindwall and Miller, Denis,' chirped one of the old school. 'Only a dab or two of Brylcreem, old boy,' he replied. He was, of course, one of the first great sporting personalities to benefit from sponsorship. But that was about the closest he came to boasting about his remarkable dual playing career, modesty being an endearing quality he shared with some of his contemporaries, like Tom Finney, Nat Lofthouse and Stanley Matthews.

Sir Stanley gave me a memorable interview in the Gresham Hotel in Dublin one morning in May 1980. The previous day he had been admitted to the Aer Lingus Hall of Fame along with Paddy Coad, an Irish sporting hero. We had just begun the interview when an ambulance, lights flashing, siren wailing, screeched to a halt under the blue canopies of the hotel. Two ambulance men rushed through the doors and over to the reception desk. We wondered if someone had collapsed.

The next moment, the two ambulance men came sprinting into the lounge where we were sitting, straight up to Sir Stanley and thrust pen and paper under his nose. The senior officer spoke. 'We're on our way to a job Sir Stanley but we'd heard you were staying here so can we have your autograph for our boys?' As they shot off down O'Connell Street, siren still wailing, I wondered if this legend of English soccer had ever signed his autograph in more bizarre circumstances or, more to the point, what happened to the poor sod who was waiting for the ambulance.

A postscript to that tale is how my token attempt at a bit of originality, in writing the feature, was totally lost on my sports editor the next day. It was Ireland, it was Dublin and, because Sir Stanley had a shock of white hair, a white polar-necked jumper and was also wearing a black leather jacket, I described him graphically and added that he 'looked as tall and cool as a glass of stout'. I didn't put 'Guinness' because it was not the *Sunday Express's* style then to advertise. The northern sports editor 'subbed' the copy, came over to my desk in our Manchester office and said 'Nice piece but I've just tickled the first par a bit. Stout is not all that popular over here, so I've changed it to lager!'

Sometimes a little can be lost in the translation. I recall when the Americans were trying to make a go of big-time soccer and the New York Cosmos signed the great German sweeper Franz Beckenbauer. A tobacco-chomping Cosmos executive, with no understanding of the game, became increasingly agitated before shouting: 'Tell the Kraut (Beckenbauer) to get his ass upfield because we aint paying a million dollars for a guy who hangs around at the back!'

And what if the brain simply doesn't engage. I was left feeling like the school dunce on a Liverpool trip to Barcelona in the late Seventies. Gaudy shirts were fashionable and I was wearing one with a giraffe pattern when Kevin Keegan walked past me in the hotel lobby. 'Did you get that shirt from Jack Charlton?' It didn't twig with me at all and Kevin walked away muttering 'I can't help it if you've got a very low IQ.'

Heh, just a minute. Some footballers are none too bright either. Everton had a real 'Bungalow' Bob in the squad Howard Kendall honed into one of the most successful in Europe in the mid-eighties. They conceded a costly goal in the closing minutes of a league game at Goodison Park when they were caught out by a deep cross, a blind-side run and volley. Amid the uproar, the captain Kevin Ratcliffe turned accusingly to another defender

Hold the front page! Another birth, death or
marriage in Harrogate.

With Martin Buchan and Alex Stepney. Two
Reds and a Blue!

The English Press team beaten 10-2 by the
French Press at Liverpool's training ground
in 1977. So much for Bill Shankly's powers
of motivation!

Eat your heart out, Elton John and Diana Ross ... I've also played to a 'full house' at Wembley Arena.

Peter Collins and family with a small selection
of his trophies. Surely the greatest British
sportsman never to receive official recognition.

With two of the more glamorous members
of the speedway fraternity, Bobbi Hunter
and Madelaine Fundin.

Ron Atkinson and John Bond – deadly rivals
at the two Manchester clubs in the 1980's
and always good for a story.

With my great pals Norman Wynne and
Don Evans, and some of the trophies won
by Northern clubs in 1985.

With two of my former sports editors!

In Italy during the 1990 World Cup – I've
just run out of Tippex for my monitor.

With another 'Sunday' pal, Vince Wilson,
wondering if the toilets at this Colosseum
place are better than at Wembley?

Alex Ferguson, the greatest of modern
managers

and demanded 'Where the hell did he come from?' The dimwit responded 'I think he's from Charlton on a free transfer!'

I believe the same Everton player went out to South Africa to consider a loan spell that summer. Some of his Goodison colleagues were surprised he was even thinking about it. He was asked on his return 'What about the Apartheid?' 'No problem, it's nice, it's got two bedrooms.'

One of Liverpool's biggest stars was being interviewed on *BBC Radio Wales* and was shocked to learn that another journalist he had known well at the start of his career, had passed away. 'He can't have been very old, what did he die of?' The radio man replied 'The Big C.' 'That's a shame ... fancy drowning when you're such a good swimmer!'

And when Rangers were drawn against a team from the Faroes in the Champions Cup, one of their players wanted to know how an Egyptian club had got into Europe.

Joey Jones, that madcap Welshman who was no fool when it came to playing against the best for Liverpool and his country, used to have his team mates in tears with his lunacy and his impersonations of people like Tommy Cooper, Michael Crawford, Eddie Waring and Max Bygraves. 'I'm as thick as that wall,' admitted Joey, 'but I'm having a great time. I've always been a loony. I once stuffed my school satchel with field mice and let them loose in the English class.'

When Wrexham sent him and his barmy pal Mickey Thomas to college, to learn a trade, they asked if they could do 'quarry-blasting'. Eventually, they were kicked out for playing table tennis with the putty, in the Painting and Decorating class.

Joey rejoined Wrexham a few years ago and I bet their young kids find him a hoot—as well as a very good coach. Mickey Thomas, the scamp who got himself caught up in a forged notes scandal after tasting the high life with Manchester United, Everton and Chelsea, has teamed up with Joey on the after-dinner circuit. Mickey brings the house down wherever they go, with his crack about 'I don't envy today's top players earning thirty grand a week. I was on that myself until the police took away my printing machine!'

A major problem players have to cope with is advice from the sidelines. In a UEFA Cup tie abroad, Liverpool's Brian Hall was positioned quite close to the dug-out when goalkeeper Ray Clemence hurled a long pass in his direction. Before the ball had reached him, five different Liverpool 'experts' bawled five different instructions from the dug-out. 'Head it' ... 'Trap it' ... 'On your chest' ... 'Pass it' ... 'Run with it.'

Sport is full of characters, many of them highly intelligent and certainly smart enough to build new careers for themselves when they finish playing. Francis Lee was a real livewire on and off the pitch in his years with Bolton, Manchester City and Derby. If the fans ever called him 'rubbish', which wasn't often, it didn't bother him because he finished up making a fortune out of waste paper—and then became a very successful racehorse trainer. Admittedly, he found it difficult to keep his impish sense of humour when he went back to City as chairman!

Frannie was such a master at falling in the box that he was nick-named 'Lee Won Pen'. In one game at Maine Road, he was on a mazy run for goal and after beating one defender suddenly grabbed his ankle, feigned mock agony and hopped for a few yards. For a split second the big centre half about to lunge at him, froze, like a rabbit caught in the headlights. It was long enough. 'Conned' hopelessly, the defender could do nothing as Frannie resumed his speedy run. That little piece of mischief was worth the admission money alone.

Many sports celebrities have established themselves on the after-dinner circuit and although the majority I know are footballers, simply because my career has taken me further down that road than any other, I have enjoyed the company of some fascinating people in other sports.

Do you remember the Oscar-winning Hollywood movie Raging Bull, which was the life story of the former teenage hoodlum and wife-beating world middleweight boxing champion Jake La Motta, played in the film by Robert de Niro? La Motta came to Manchester a few years ago to entertain at a boxing dinner at Bredbury Hall. I caught up with him that afternoon and, believe me, even at 66 he was an awesome presence. And the one-liners would have done Groucho Marx proud. 'I have a great personality ... I can light up a room just by leaving it ... My sixth wife and I are totally compatible. When we go to bed we both have headaches at the same time ... In six fights with Sugar Ray Robinson he never knocked me down. Only my wives had me off my feet.'

I saw David Watkins, one of the great halfbacks of Welsh rugby union, successfully switch to rugby league with Salford and asked him later if he had been given a tough baptism. He replied 'In my first game for Salford, I was so quick it took the other team a while to catch me. Then this massive second row forward grabbed me, turned me upside down and dropped me on his knee like he was breaking a twig. And he said "Now let's see you twinkle, twinkle little bloody star".'

Of all the cricketers I have encountered, I particularly remember an interview with the then Yorkshire fast bowler Tony Nicholson at Barnsley. It was 13 years to the day since he had broken into the Yorkshire side and he recalled the words of the legendary F. S. Trueman on that occasion.

'He came across to me and said "Nathen lad, you're No 28" and I said "What do you mean, I'm battin' eleven?" And Trueman said "Nay, I mean you're 28th to oppen bowlin' wi me—and if you've nowt to offer I'll see you off like all t'rest".'

Sometimes it is hard to win the trust of a person you have never met previously. I had a few problems with Barry Wood, the cricket all-rounder who did such a splendid job for Derbyshire after leaving Lancashire. Eventually he agreed to be interviewed, in the pavilion at Chesterfield, and I produced my tape recorder.

We talked for half an hour and there was nothing contentious but Barry wanted to see a copy of the finished article. Fair enough. I got a bit pissed off when he then asked for the tape as well, once I'd made a transcript. 'No way,' I said. 'Why not?' he asked, suspiciously. 'Because it's got Neil Sedaka on the other side!'

Little Harry Pilling, the pint-sized Lancashire batsman, was no easy target for bowlers. He told me how the Kent seamer Alan Brown rapped him on the pad and appealed for lbw. 'Not out' said the umpire, 'it was too high.' 'Too high?' exclaimed Brown in disgust, 'if it had hit him on the head he'd still have been plum!'

Years ago I used to report on those Dinner and Boxing nights at the Anglo-American Sporting Club in Manchester's Piccadilly Hotel. The lads had to sit in a hotel room on the seventh floor until the dinner and raffle and speeches were over and it was often round midnight before the last pair got into the ring. Most of the boxers, with no disrespect, were newcomers or no-hopers. I had a bit of a problem one night with a light heavyweight from Bootle who sat on the bed, gloved up and ready to fight two hours before he was called. All I wanted was some biog but I couldn't understand what he was saying because he wouldn't remove his gum-shield!

Tennis, at its best, is a wonderful game and I like watching the flair players, the entertainers. But tell me something. Was Henri Le Conte a name or a description?

Back to soccer and one of the best of the after-dinner brigade is Duncan McKenzie, whose party piece in his days with Nottingham Forest, Leeds, Everton and others, was to jump over a Mini motor car. 'These days I'm lucky to get a jump in one,' he says. 'Dunc' used to team up with Liverpool's Welsh international John Toshack on *BBC Radio Merseyside* and it became a cult show. Their speciality was the hoax celebrity interview.

'It all started when Bill Shankly was due to come on the programme,' said Duncan. 'Unfortunately, he had to cry off at the last minute. We had billed him—pardon the pun—so Tosh decided to imitate Shanks while I played it straight as the interviewer. He did it so well, we got away with it. The next week Liverpool were playing Barcelona in the UEFA Cup so we did a skit interview with Tosh as Johann Cruyff, using special sound effects to make it seem like an authentic long-distance call. Happy days.'

Duncan thoroughly enjoys public speaking, particularly the after-dinner scene. 'Some people get very nervous but I love doing it. You don't have to be a Bernard Manning or a Norman Collier to make people laugh. They love hearing stories about the game's personalities. Not just football speakers, either. Gordon Brown from rugby union, Billy Thompson the former rugby league referee, David Lloyd and Geoff Miller from cricket are all very good.'

And if you want to hear a hundred sporting voices on the same night, try to catch Kevin Connolly, the best impressionist in the business.

Steve Kindon, another top raconteur, cracked me up when I interviewed him years ago when he was a barnstorming winger at Burnley. He came out with lines like 'I've got the speed of a racehorse, the work-rate of a drayhorse and the brains of a rocking horse! I've also been described as a runaway wardrobe!'

Mick Quinn, the former Portsmouth, Newcastle and Coventry striker, is another wag who is never short of a story or a punch-line. 'Sumo', as the fans used to call him, had a spell with the Greek club PAOK Salonika and made his debut in a cup tie away from home. 'In the first minute I did what I used to do in England. I clattered the opposing goalkeeper. He went down clutching his face and the next thing someone kicked me from behind, another pulled my hair, a third punched me to the ground. As I got up someone spat in my face and another ground his studs into the back of my hand. That's when things started to turn a bit nasty!'

As they did for my old pal Barry Diamond in a Fourth Division game for Halifax Town away to Cambridge United in August 1986. Do you remember Barry? I mentioned him in the opening chapter.

It was only the third game of the season but the day was wet and miserable and the Abbey Stadium pitch very slippy. Barry is not a big lad but he was playing centre forward for Halifax and 'mixing it' with a typically Neanderthal defender.

'I've always been a bit fiery and we were at it from the start, kicking lumps out of each other. But in the second half he caught me with a really nasty tackle and we both went down in a heap. Next thing, the ref runs over with his notebook open and pencil poised. It was before they brought back the red and yellow cards.

'I can't remember his name but he was the first coloured ref I'd ever seen. Well, for a moment I thought I was down the local Indian restaurant and I couldn't resist it. I just grinned at him and said "Three curries and a shish kebab, please." And he did us both ... the centre half for the foul and me for a racist remark. The Cambridge lad couldn't get up for laughing.

'We lost 1-0 so when we got back to our dressing room our manager Mick Jones wasn't in the mood for jokes. But he was puzzled. "That was diabolical. How come you got booked as well?" I said "Dissent, boss." So he said "Dissent? When he clattered you? What did you say?". "Three curries and a shish kebab".

'The lads cracked up and the manager went potty. It was a club fine if you were booked for dissent, so it cost me twenty-five per cent of my wages ... which was about £3.50. But you've got to laugh, haven't you?

'Look, I'm not a racist, I just like a laugh. And the best part was waiting for the referee's report. Normally, if you called someone "a black bastard" the ref put it in his report. I couldn't wait to see "Three curries and a shish kebab" on the form. But the ref just put "racial dissent." He bottled it.'

Alfie Buksh, a splendid referee from London, was the official concerned. Now retired, I hope he doesn't feel it necessary to reach for the yellow card again!

Fourteen

DIRECTORS

FOOTBALL directors are a much-maligned breed, which is something I feel honour-bound to say because several of them have been particularly hospitable to me down the years.

There was a time when clubs from top to bottom of the social scale enjoyed a much more fraternal relationship with the various branches of the media than they do now, inviting us to share their triumphs and their disappointments. Banquets, parties, wakes.

If you travelled with Liverpool, when they were at their all-conquering best in Europe, the chances were you had a glass of champagne in your hand before take-off. Maybe even a bottle. And that was on the outward flight. You could say, Liverpool were different glass!

Well, nearly as good as Rochdale, my local club, who have managed to laugh in the face of adversity for generations and become famous for their hospitality the length and breadth of the land.

I have always fancied being a football club director when the ink in my pen finally runs dry or my computer goes down. For all the wrong reasons, I suppose. Comfort, ego, whisky. What's that ... how big is my interest-free loan going to be? Forget it!

Some of my best friends are chairmen or directors and their commitment, both financial and in time and energy, has to be commended. They are not all lucky enough to sit in upholstered luxury at Old Trafford, Anfield or Highbury watching the high-profile cosmopolitan Premier League.

Rochdale used to have a framed photograph in their boardroom of the summer's day their ground was used for a cattle auction. The chairman and then vice chairman were pictured looking down from the directors' box at an assortment of cattle leaving their deposits on the pitch. Whenever a visiting VIP queried the wisdom of the exercise, the retort was a hoot. 'We have to watch a load of s*** on the pitch all winter so why not in the summer?'

David Kilpatrick, the granite merchant who has chaired the Rochdale board through thin and thin and is one of the most gregarious fellows you could wish to meet, believes it is time Rochdale stopped encouraging people to laugh at them.

The club has come a long way, in terms of respectability on and off the field and structural redevelopment, from the days when they had to apply for re-election almost annually and when a bucket had to be placed in the boardroom because the roof leaked.

It irritates him that Rochdale are still ridiculed as the extreme alternative to the Manchester Uniteds of this world and has told me, pointedly: 'We don't want a reputation for our pies, we want promotion!'

So did Fred Ratcliffe, back in the 70's when only his cash and 'old pals' network kept Rochdale in the Football League. The thanks he got for pulling the club back from the brink one year, was a knife in the back. I was sitting next to one of his fellow-directors at a dinner to mark Fred's 25th year as chairman. As Fred got up to respond to the tributes, his boardroom 'colleague' whispered: 'This club will never go anywhere until we get rid of that old bugger.' It would have gone out of existence, that's where it would have gone.

A man who loved the club with such a passion that he propped it up for years and then danced on the bar counter in the supporters' club until three in the morning, when the 'Dale' knocked First Division Coventry City out of the FA Cup in 1971, deserved more respect than that.

So do all directors who put their heart and soul and cheque-book into a club, even if some of them talk through their backsides half the time. They don't help their case when stories like this abound. CHAIRMAN: (frostily, to his manager after another defeat and with their relationship and the club's league position already at rock bottom): 'I've told you before ... pick Harrison.' MANAGER: 'I did. He was left back.' CHAIRMAN: 'Then drop him—he was useless.'

The last thing a manager wants is a chairman who interferes, who thinks he knows more about the game than the man appointed to do the job, who wants to pick the team and give team talks but would never take the rap for a bad result.

Worse still is a chairman who wants to play! There was one around in the lower divisions, who used to 'kick in' with the team before a game and even threatened to pick himself once the promotion and relegation issues had been resolved. I don't suppose the little matter of a 'player's registration' entered his thoughts; only winning his silly bet.

And do you remember Michael Knighton, when he 'bought' Manchester United for £10 million in August 1989, running out in track-suit top, shorts and boots before the opening game of the season against Arsenal at Old Trafford? We couldn't believe what we were seeing. He juggled the ball on his head, blew kisses to the bewildered crowd and 'scored' three times at the Stretford End. I suppose, for a day or three, the biggest club in the land was his train set.

At his press conference the previous day, when Mr Knighton was at his most animated, the millionaire property developer came out with an astonishing generalisation that 'football is a team effort and, with all due respect, a monkey could manage a successful football team.' I don't think he said it in earshot of Alex Ferguson.

I would be the last to suggest that Mr Knighton proved his point by effectively becoming the manager of Carlisle United himself after sacking Mervyn Day, who took them up from the

Third Division. How could he, when Carlisle were singularly unsuccessful on the pitch. But at least this eccentric chairman recognised the players. There have been a number of reported instances of young soccer writers being mistaken for players by directors and wondering how to respond to 'Well done, excellent game' or 'Great save from that penalty, lad.'

Joe Royle told me a 'classic' about the manager of a Third Division club who presented his directors with his 'retained list' at the end of a moderately-successful season.

The directors examined the list; there were a few gasps of surprise and indignation and then, after going into a huddle, the chairman rose from his seat.

'We can't understand, manager, why you are proposing to give a free transfer to our centre half and captain who our own supporters have voted the club's "Player of the Year". And he's a good lad, by all accounts.'

The manager had prepared himself for such a reaction and countered: 'I take your point, chairman, but the problem is our centre half is too small. He's only five foot nine and if we are ever going to get out of this division, we need more height in that position. Also, at 33 the best chance of getting him off the wage bill is to give him a "free".'

Again the club's directors went into a huddle before the chairman, like the foreman of a jury, rose to his feet again. 'WE like this player and think he's good for the team. So would it help if his boots were fitted with longer studs and insoles to make him taller?'

The manager stood there open-mouthed in disbelief when, suddenly, one of the other directors piped up: 'That's the most stupid bloody idea I've ever heard.' Just when the manager thought 'thank God they're not all idiots,' the director added: 'The FA would never allow it!'

It was the legendary England inside forward Len Shackleton who perpetuated the myth, that football directors are all candidates for the chairmanship of the 'Know-nowt-about-it club', with his blank page in his autobiography under the heading 'What the average football club director knows about football'. It caused a furore in the Fifties.

'Shack' lost none of his mischievousness when he joined the *Sunday People* as a reporter and columnist. When Northampton shot up through the divisions and faced Sunderland, one of his old clubs, he wrote: 'Northampton, the town where they make boots and shoes, brought their own brand of clog to Roker Park.' And he was scathing about one player in particular. 'He kept being caught off balance when his team mates passed the ball to his wrong FEET!'

But directors were his pet target and even now they are often regarded by managers, players and fans as 'wooden-tops', which gives an amusing slant to the perennial cry 'Sack the board.'

The bottom line is that you don't need a vast knowledge of the game to become the director of a football/rugby/cricket/ etc club. Better still, don't have a bottom line; just deep pockets. Professional sport is such big business, so money-orientated now that any old millionaire who comes along wanting to buy a club, hardly makes a dent in the annual wage bill. To throw money at a club these days you need to enlist the help of a battalion of discus and javelin champions and/or the stock market. For 'Joe Public' read 'Go Public'.

Brian Clough once said that football clubs attract a certain percentage of 'nobodies who want to be somebodies' and he was spot on. Some of the free-loaders who are last out of the boardroom on match days wouldn't buy a round in their local at Christmas. (We've got some like that in the press room, too!) They also tend to go AWOL when results on the field take a turn for the worse. You wouldn't expect to see empty seats in the Directors Box at Old Trafford or Anfield but I've seen it happen.

Most directors are highly successful, often self-made, businessmen but how many apply their business nous when it comes to football? They are guilty of taking some outrageous gambles which more often than not plunge the club even deeper into debt. Could it have something to do with ego? As my old pal Freddie Pye, former chairman of Stockport and Wigan, vice chairman of Manchester City and now of Sheffield United, told me years ago: 'No one wants to be a director of the club at the bottom of the league. The game has gone potty. It is being crucified by greed and we must take the blame for allowing transfer fees to spiral and for paying silly money to players. We stand for it because we are ambitious and egotistical.

'Players demand more and more. Signing on fees, loyalty bonuses, win bonuses, draw bonuses, crowd bonuses, appearance money. And that's just when you want someone on a "free". Appearance money, for God sake? I said to one player "Do you mean to tell me you might not appear? What are you, a bloody magician?" Money is pouring out of the game and it's all going down a tunnel marked "players".

'I am sick of directors being made the fall guys. I have been a director for years and have personally guaranteed fortunes. So have dozens of other football club directors around the country. It's about time the players accepted some responsibility for the rising cost of football. Where would the game be without directors? Who do they think signs the guarantees at the bank? Where do they think the money comes from?'

These days it just falls out of the *Sky*, golden rain from satellite television; millions of pounds per season, supplemented by kit sponsorships, marketing and perimeter advertising. And, if the club is big enough to go public, another windfall drops into their bank balances. As for the rest, the majority ... well, something far less pleasant continues to fall on them from a great height.

While the rich get richer, the poor struggle to keep the bailiffs and receivers from the door—Bournemouth and Brighton are recent examples—and numerous others before them. Out of the frying pan into the VAT, so to speak.

One of the strangest cost-cutting exercises I witnessed was when four directors from Hartlepool United shared a table with Rochdale and Leeds at what used to be called the FLESA (Football League Executive Staffs Association) Dinner in a posh London hotel in the early 80's. During the meal one of the Hartlepool lads kept keeling over for a few seconds and then sitting upright again. I thought he was having a cardiac arrest. Suddenly, he caught my eye, grinned and asked 'Want a Scotch? Gin? Vodka?' He had a supermarket bag under the table full of bottles of spirits and kept leaning over to pour one for his mates when the waiters had their backs turned. 'You don't think we are going to pay their bloody prices, do you?'

I have long had a soft spot for Manchester City and their capacity to shoot themselves in the foot or even more tender parts of their anatomy. Frannie Lee dubbed them the club that could win cups for cock-ups when he was there as a player in the glory years.

Frannie was in the 1969 FA Cup-winning side and remembers the old chairman Albert Alexander going into the dressing room after City had beaten Everton in the semi finals, at Villa Park, and saying 'Well done lads. Now we are going to Wembley and we're going to make a lot of money and then we can buy some better players!' Frannie gambled plenty on coming back as chairman a few years ago and I know there are times when he wishes he hadn't bothered.

The late Peter Swales was ousted to make way for Frannie's consortium and it was a nasty chapter in the club's history, more like a military coup than a take-over. But even Swales, who I had known for more than twenty years and seen rise from non-league football to chairman of the Football Association international committee, admitted he had overstayed his welcome.

In his early days at Maine Road, as a trouble shooter, he had a reputation for sacking anyone who didn't say 'Good morning' and we had a few run-ins over articles in the *Sunday*

Express that he didn't like. He took exception to one during a pre-season trip to Huelva in southern Spain, causing a scene in the hotel and then 'treating' me to a tumbler of Bacardi by way of mock apology.

He made the waiter keep pouring until there was hardly any room for the coke. I didn't want it anyway because I'd had a few beers in the afternoon, but he insisted. We were just about to leave for a game against Atletico Madrid, in the local stadium a mile up the road, and Swales even kept the manager Tony Book and the City players waiting, insisting I had to finish my drink. Then he decided the coach could leave but that we should walk to the ground in the 100 degrees heat. It was a kind of childish battle of wills.

I remember walking up the road with Peter Gardner of the *Manchester Evening News* and starting to perspire and stagger in the heat. 'Keep going, we're nearly there,' said Gardner. 'If you can hold out, you've cracked it from now on.' It was more by luck than judgement, I can tell you, but just as we reached the stadium I saw a couple of beer stalls. Mind you, I was seeing two of everything by then. I turned to Swales. 'My turn to buy you one, Peter.' He was caught off his guard, momentarily. 'Er ... Sorry, I need to go in to meet the officials. Next time.' Believe it or not but after that episode we became quite good friends. Instead of Bacardi he fed me some great stories, some about City, some on England trips, and I had lunch with him only a fortnight before he died in 1996.

Funnily enough, I also remember that trip to Huelva for an example of how Peter Swales charmed his way out of an embarrassing situation. Clearly, City had under-estimated the status of the competition because when the host club, Huelva, held a lavish reception for the four competing clubs, City, Atletico Madrid, Partizan Belgrade and Real Betis of Seville, it was televised live. And Swales suddenly realised the chairmen or presidents of the other clubs planned to exchange expensive gifts; magnificent cut-glass vases and carved club crests.

Swales made frantic gestures from the dais to other City officials and they rustled up some badges and pennants. Big deal! But when it came to Swales's turn to reciprocate he did it with such flamboyance and style and made such a brilliant tub-thumping speech, punching the air at the finish, that he won the biggest ovation of the lot.

Another chairman who made an indelible mark on me was the infamous Burnley butcher Bob Lord. For twenty years his bulldog's bark had reverberated along the corridors of English football and all but emptied the Turf Moor press box. Anyone who wrote a wrong word, he banned. It reached a point where if you were banned, you qualified for a special tie.

When the main stand was demolished and the press had to be temporarily re-housed, the box was put right at the back of the big new stand behind the goal and in the far left hand corner, overlooking the corner flag. It made identi-fication of players at the far end of the pitch almost impossible on murky days and nights and the regulars took to taking binoculars.

Eric Todd, former distinguished football correspondent of *The Guardian*, informed his readers that it was possible to see the village of Portsmouth from this crow's nest vantage point and that if it had been much higher he could have seen Portsmouth in Hampshire. Believe it or not, the current press box, in the new stand, is even higher.

Old Bob didn't care what the press thought but he mellowed. He was 70 and in his 24th year as Burnley's chairman when I finally got him to agree to be interviewed and admitted he was growing old and tired. 'I might have been a rebel once, not now,' he said. 'Much of the time I was a voice in the wilderness. I could be rude, I admit that—but only if people were rude to me. I banned some of the people in your profession because they took advantage of me being controversial and they hurt this club. Well this club is like my own family and if anyone hurts my family I take a stick to them!'

Former Burnley star Steve Kindon tells a story about how he had to make a speech at a function and how Bob Lord, who was sitting next to him, said 'Just remember to stand up, speak up and shut up.' At that moment, Mrs Lord leaned across and said, dryly 'You were never able to get past the first two, were you Bob?'

Fifteen

FANS

IF we discount the head-bangers and professional trouble-makers, who could start a fight in an empty house, the rest of us are all fans at heart—even fickle hacks like me who jump from one bandwagon to the next during the football or cricket season. You can do that when you work for the 'nationals' whereas the poor provincial evening guys, or even district sports writers on the dailies and 'Sundays', betray their colours. They practically fall on their swords in anguish in the press box when their teams go out of the FA Cup or the NatWest Trophy.

You've got to remember, that defeat might have cost them their one and only chance of a trip to Wembley, Lord's or into Europe the following season. But, take it from me, we all have an allegiance to some sport and most of us to one club somewhere. That result we look for when we are miles away from home. In fact, the club in question might be miles away.

One of my 'Sunday' rivals in Manchester was always a tormented soul until he heard how Brighton and Hove Albion had gone on. You can imagine how close he has been to topping himself these last few seasons. At least he cares. I can't believe life has become so insipid that any self-respecting sports writer drifts from game to game like a gypsy with amnesia.

Down the years, at various times, I have pledged my support to Neilston Juniors, Arthurlie, St Mirren, Rangers, Portsmouth, Guildford City, Harrogate Town, Bradford Park Avenue, Leeds United, Coventry City, Wolverhampton Wanderers, Doncaster Rovers, Manchester United, Manchester

City and Rochdale. Sounds a bit like midnight at Euston Station
or the song *Last train to San Fernando!* Fifteen clubs, the last
two in tandem for twenty years or so. I'm sure the word impostor
has crossed your mind already.

But when you move around Britain so much in your youth
and your working life, clubs you once wept for no longer hold
you under their spell. Each one is a closed door, save for the last
two. And what a spring double they make! 'We'll win f*** all
again'.

Neilston Juniors, in the Scottish Junior League, were the
first team I ever saw in the flesh. My father, who worked in
Glasgow during World War Two, used to take me on the bus
from Nitshill, where we lived. He soon got fed up but I would
have stuck with Neilston if I hadn't needed an escort, so I
switched my allegiance to another junior club, Arthurlie, when
I reached the ripe old age of six. Arthurlie played just round the
corner from my primary school in Barrhead. I soon learned
that if you didn't want to get beaten up twice or 'brayed'—as
they say in Scotland—you had to support Rangers or Celtic.
Easy. Rangers were the Scotland national team in disguise and
I suppose being a protestant helped me make up my mind. St
Mirren? Well, they were just the local Scottish League club and
I went to see them once.

Guildford City are no more—the by-pass running where
the red and whites used to play—and neither is my passion for
Leeds United, the only club that really got inside my soul.
Bradford Park Avenue flirted briefly with my affections, when
we first moved to Harrogate, in 1949, but I never really fancied
them. The bus ride —referred to elsewhere—was a 'killer' and
the boring fart who chaperoned me always said the same thing,
week in week out, when the whistle blew after the first 45
minutes. 'Good half.'

So, when 'Avenue' were knocked out of the FA Cup by
Leeds in 1952, and I discovered the journey from Harrogate to
Elland Road—train to Holbeck then walk—was infinitely more

comfortable than by bone-jarring S-s-s-s-amuel Ledgaaaaaard, I changed my colours again. Foolish boy. There were shades of the Manchester City of today in the Leeds of the early and mid-fifties. You couldn't even trust them to lose. This, of course, was pre-Revie.

Do you know, 'my' Leeds were knocked out of the FA Cup three years running, in 1956, 57 and 58, in the same round, on the same ground, by the same club and by the same score. Third round, Cardiff City at home, lost 1-2. Now is that a recurring nightmare or what?

I was on the Gelderd Road terraces for all three of those catastrophes and I swear when it got to 2-1 in the third game, the fans left in droves. 'We' had a centre forward called Bob Forrest, a willing Jock, but when he shot wide or over the bar for the umpteenth time in one game a wag shouted 'Aim for the church.' I don't know what he meant but everyone in earshot laughed.

There was some good banter on the terraces at Elland Road before the 'hoolies' moved in. I was in my usual spot, close to the front wall, when the ball bobbed in and out of play monotonously in much the same area. Every Leeds player was so tightly marked at each throw-in, the defenders were heading the ball straight back out of play. The frustration was only relieved when, just as Eric Kerfoot shaped to take yet another throw, a voice shouted 'Honour your partners and let's dozey-do.'

The best terrace humour is spontaneous, and often funnier when one fan reacts to another even though they have never met. Brian Flynn, that perky bundle of Welsh energy who is the manager of Wrexham, recalls 'In one of our games, this particular player on the opposing side was making a real meal of it every time he was tackled, rolling all over the place in mock agony. Suddenly a voice shouted "You fake it better than my missus." Immediately, another voice piped up "And I can vouch for that, boyo".'

One of the more amusing letters I received at the *Sunday Express* was from a reader in Suffolk, who took me to task for not recognising that Ipswich Town had once been champions of the Football League. It was dated 'Pay Day' and delightfully written in dialect, as follows:

'Mr Bott, sir.

I were a stuffing up an 'ole in our barn when I seed your bit abaht Mr Wark and the Ipswich football. Us all know as ow they won the FA Cup and us all know as ow they won that Eur, UFE, er foreign cup. But it seems loike as ow sum on us doant know as ow we also won the First Division. But then, o'course, yew doant come from these ere parts, dew yew boy?

Respectful loike,
Owd Adams'

My allegiance to Leeds probably waned about the time the legendary John Charles went off to play for Juventus. And, of course, when my own circumstances changed and I left home for the first time and went to work in Coventry. From then on, wherever the job took me, Birmingham, Wolverhampton, Doncaster and Manchester, so I cast one off and picked up another. And in Manchester, it was United first and then City, which is I suppose the way it will always be, whether I like it or not.

When I saw United win the European Cup in '68 I thought they were the 'bees knees'. But over the years I have made more friends at Maine Road, done some work for the club, seen my son Julian grow up a City fan because United did nothing to 'catch' him when City had the 'Junior Blues', and generally had a softer spot for the mad, enigmatic, self-destructive, our-day-will-come-but-God-knows-when Blues.

I'm not a true Blue because I can derive pleasure from watching United, particularly in Europe, and I switch to neutral when I am 'on duty'. Some can't. Some of my press colleagues are so unashamedly red they should live in pillar boxes. But at least they observe the unwritten rule that a press box is a place of work and people don't jump up and start screaming 'GOAAAAALL!' We leave the banshee impressions to the radio men.

The discipline comes from training the mind to go into rewind mode to establish the source and route of the move leading up to the goal. Believe it or not, very few press boxes, even in the Carling Premier League, have television monitors to provide action replays.

Dear old City are one of the few clubs who do provide this facility but even they managed to cock it up the first time it was used, a couple of seasons back. The TV was suspended above the press seats. Unfortunately, it had been tuned in to the wrong channel and we had to sit there watching the game against a noisy background of Tele Savalas and *The Dirty Dozen*.

There is only one place to be a real football fan and that's in the crowd. Not in the press box, not in a glass-fronted, centrally-heated, champagne-swilling executive box, not even in the padded comfort of the Directors' Box, not in the pub, not at home in front of the TV but there, live, on the day, in the crowd.

Many a night, when I haven't been required to do a match report, I have stood on the terraces where they still 'survive' and shouted along with the rest. Most of the humour these days is confined to chants and song parodies. Samples: 'We'll score again, don't know where, don't know when but I know we'll score again some sunny day' ... 'We're so crap it's unbelievable' ... 'There's only one greedy bastard, one greedy baass-taard' ... 'You only sing when you're fishing, sing when you're fish-ing' ... 'He shot, he missed, he must be f****** pissed, Andy Cole, Andy Cole'.

That last one has gone for a bowl of cherries. Well done, Coley!

The increasing popularity of one-day cricket means that most matches are accompanied by well-lubricated football-style chants like 'Oh Lanky Lanky, Lanky-lanky-lanky-lanky-Lancashire' or 'There's only one Devon Malcolm, one Devon Maal-colm'. But if you play cricket in pyjamas and all that jazz, and let the lager flow all day, you get the crowd you deserve.

Occasionally, you can still unearth a verbal nugget. Rochdale used to have a striker called Alan Young, who had known better days and bigger clubs and now couldn't even hold down a place at Spotland. To be fair, he'd had a few injuries but it appeared that he was just going through the motions to see out his contract.

He was on the bench for this particular night match and, after half an hour, dragged himself to his feet, ambled a few yards along the touchline, did a couple of stretching exercises and then sat down again. 'Heh, Youngie,' bawled a voice from the terraces, 'That your training done for another week?' Even the manager liked that one.

On another night at Spotland, which Brian Green, one of Rochdale's ex-managers once described as 'a cemetery with lights', which is probably one reason for the 'ex', the then incumbent Dave Sutton was indulging in a bit of 'manager-speak'. You know the sort of stuff. 'Getting good balls in' ... 'playing in the last third of the pitch' ... 'closing down'.

Whatever Rochdale's No 4 was doing, he wasn't doing it right for 'Sutty', who bawled from the bench 'Heh, Reidy, I've told you before ... stick it in the channel'.

A voice from the terraces hollered 'I've heard of a 'long ball' but that's bleedin' ridiculous!'

Rugby league crowds are great sources of wit. Years ago I was standing behind the posts at Salford when the Red Devils were playing Leeds. Salford had just scored a try and while the Leeds players waited for the conversion attempt, one of them, the Great Britain winger Alan Smith, turned and glared at the home fans. With his teeth out, he wasn't a pretty sight. 'Heh, Smithy,' came the cry. 'I bet you were a bloody ugly baby!' Could it have been our friend from Rochdale?

On another occasion at Salford, one of the deep-throated home fans roared menacingly 'Get that black bastard!' Suddenly, one of Salford's big forwards whirled round and the fan's voice changed to falsetto as he whimpered 'No, not you Colin (Dixon), I meant their black bastard!'

Racism will always exist in sport but it needn't be a problem unless it is malicious. Dave Barends, a Bantu warrior who used to play for Bradford Northern (now the Bradford Bulls), happily tells a story against himself.

He was playing for Bradford against Hull at The Boulevard on a filthy night when the rain was tipping down. A Hull player launched an 'up and under' and Dave 'lost' it in the floodlights. Suddenly, the white ball landed on his bald pate and bounced into the crowd, whereupon a Humberside wag shouted 'In off the black, seven away!'

The use of video action replays in resolving contentious issues has worked well in rugby league and cricket. If it comes into soccer, how long before we hear the fans chant 'the video's a wanker'?

Fanzine titles can be very funny and original. Surely one of the best has to be 'There's only one F in Fulham'. Others that have tickled my fancy along the way have included 'Look back in Amber' (Hull City), 'And Smith must score' (Brighton and Hove Albion) and 'Dial M for Merthyr' (no identification needed).

One way of identifying which part of the country you are in, as if you didn't know anyway, is by listening to the tannoy announcements. Where else but Blackburn Rovers could I have been the day the tannoy blared the message: 'Would Mr Albert Clegg of Darwen please go home immediately. His whippet has just had pups.'

Newspapers, notably the tabloids, bandy words like 'crisis' and 'tragedy' when a club loses three games on the trot or someone misses a penalty. It doesn't leave them an awful lot for when they really need them, to describe genuine catastrophes like Heysel, Hillsborough and the Bradford City fire. Innocent fans, loyal fans, young and old fans, died in those appalling disasters and not all the culprits were the hooligans in their ranks. Others, who should have known better, had plenty to answer for.

I was at Heysel on that dreadful night in Brussels, Wednesday May 29 1985, when rioting led to a wall collapsing in one corner of the dilapidated old stadium shortly before the scheduled kick off for the European Cup Final between Liverpool, the holders, and Juventus. The sound of crumbling masonry, the terrified screams and the lifeless bodies laid out behind the main stand are memories that will haunt me forever. I saw more than most because I was one of the last to leave the Press Room before the game, just a few minutes after the wall gave way. Nothing could have prepared me for the horror of it all.

Thirty-eight fans died and hundreds more were injured. Liverpool's proud reputation as European ambassadors was wrecked by the folly of a few and English clubs were barred from playing abroad as a result. Yet, only the previous week, I had been in Rotterdam to see Everton play Austria Vienna in the final of the Cup Winners Cup and fans of both clubs had played street football together while Dutch police applauded the cameraderie.

Hooliganism, vandalism, racial prejudice, anger, verbal and physical abuse will never be eradicated totally, because of the world we live in today, but the success of Euro 96 emphasised that progress has been made in the right direction. The steel fences have gone, along with much of the terracing, old stadiums have been revamped and fine new ones built. Family enclosures. The success of the Football in the Community scheme pioneered by the PFA. Progress, undeniably, but at a price and not merely financial.

It is important to end on a lighter note if only because that is what being a fan should be about. Involvement, passion and enjoyment, regardless of colour, class or creed. When cricket's World Cup was played in India there was no bigger match than when the host nation faced Pakistan. Because it was to be played at night under floodlights, a European correspondent asked one of the locals 'Will there be a lot of dew in the ground?' The reply was 'Oh, no, only Muslim.'

Sixteen

SPONSORS

THERE is nothing like a good 'freebie' and paradoxically sport provides a perfect platform for companies and organisations, like *Bass*, to spend millions of pounds on sponsorship and brand-name promotion and, in so doing, do a wonderful job for the beer, wine and spirits industry.

Sports writers frequently benefit from being invited to receptions, lunches and press conferences when they often drink more than they would buy in a week.

Terry Brindle, former cricket correspondent of *The Yorkshire Post*, coined a delightful phrase when he summed up a visit to the *Cornhill Insurance* tent at a Test match with the words 'We are sponsored as newts.'

I know the feeling. It never pours but it rains. Wet afternoons at cricket when the covers are on and there is nothing better to do than linger in the sponsor's marquee. Looking for a story, of course! And how many VIP's in the Tented Village at The Open Golf Championship actually go out onto the course and watch the play, rain or shine?

Executive suites and hospitality boxes are all the rage since professional sport decided to go up-market but all that pampered treatment can cushion you from the real world. I had a 'busman's holiday' a couple of years ago, wined and dined in luxury by *Thistle Hotels* in one of the private boxes in Leeds United's towering East Stand. They were playing Manchester United, the old enemy from across the Pennines.

It was jackets off and plenty of Beaujolais, bonhomie and may-the-best-team-win in the box, warmed by the central heating and the red wine. Then, with kick-off time approaching, we slid back the glass partition to take our seats to be met by an atmosphere that was as chilling as the night air. It was like walking into a bearpit.

It's not quite the same shock to the system at a big cricket match, in fact I can't think of a more idyllic way to spend a day than at a *Cornhill Insurance* Test match or a *Texaco* Trophy one-day international, provided the sun is high in the sky and the play is riveting. Thanks to two good friends, Ian Corner and Martin Orme, the respective general managers of the Portland Thistle and The Copthorne, two of Manchester's top hotels, I have savoured the experience more than once.

One of the best social gatherings of the season in football used to be the *Bell's Whisky* Manager of the Year lunch, which was held alternately in Glasgow and London on the eve of the England-Scotland international. The very first one I went to, in Glasgow, was an education. Instead of having a different wine with every course, they had a different vintage of *Bell's Whisky*, starting with the day-to-day stuff and moving into dreamland through the malts.

The guests, mostly media and managers, sat informally at round tables with a *Bell's* rep, in a green blazer, as host. By the time they had completed the divisional awards and got round to the actual Manager of the Year, there seemed to be TWO of them!

Everyone who attended one of those luncheons was given a *Bell's Whisky* Manager of the Year tie, embroidered with the logo and the year, as a souvenir. And I had some fun with them, I can tell you. Fans around the country were well aware of the awards and most of the winners were household names, e.g. Brian Clough, Bob Paisley, Howard Kendall, Kenny Dalglish. So you can imagine the puzzled looks on people's faces if they saw me at a match wearing a *Bell's* Manager of the Year tie.

If they were pleasant and said 'Oh, you're the manager of Reading, aren't you? Or is it Gillingham?' Or they asked politely how I came to have one of the ties, I was happy to explain. But, occasionally, I got some stroppy sod who looked down his nose at me and said '*Bell's* Manager of the Year? Never seen you before in me life. What you do, nick it?'

If I chose to ignore him, he'd persist. 'Go on then ... which bloody club you won it for?' By now I had the drill 'off pat'. 'Plough Inn, Salford Sunday League, Division Eight, AM! CHAMPIONS!' You should have seen how his attitude changed. 'Bloody hell, Bell's put it abaht a bit, don't they? Thought they only did t'Football League. Do you get any dosh as well ast tie?' 'Of course,' I'd reply. 'Hundred quid and a case of scotch.' 'Bloooddy he-l-l-l-l!'

I've also had a bit of fun with a New Zealand Football Association tie, given to me by one of their officials when I was in Wellington with Graham Taylor's England in 1991. I would have had even more if I could get the accent right!

'Freebie' ties can have a 'down' side, particularly if you are wearing a blazer or, in my case, a plain blue jacket. I was driving up to the north east on a busy Saturday morning a couple of seasons ago, to cover a Newcastle United game, and stopped for a late breakfast at one of the motorway service stations.

I was wearing a dark blue tie with a *Brother* (sponsors of Manchester City) logo and, after collecting my bacon and eggs, found a corner table. A supervisor came over and said 'Don't you know you are entitled to a discount if you're a coach driver?' I spluttered indignantly that I wasn't a coach driver and didn't require a discount 'thank you'—and moved to another table. Almost immediately, a family parked themselves at the next table and one of the toddlers wandered in my direction. Next thing, the mother said 'Leave the bus driver alone to have his breakfast in peace.' The blue jacket and the *Brother* tie went to the parish jumble sale the following week.

The last *Bell's* luncheon was a lavish 'do' at The Savoy, in London, in 1988, before *Barclays Bank* took over the awards and, more recently, *Carling*. Unfortunately, for us, the Manager of the Year lunch has become a bit of a private affair since the managers formed their own association.

The northern branch of the Football Writers Association also have an annual Managers Awards 'do', at Manchester's Portland Thistle Hotel, and *Carling* have taken over the sponsorship of our big night, succeeding *Sharp Electronics*, *McEwan-Younger*, *Littlewoods*, *Guinness* and *Barclays Bank*. We are indebted to all of them for helping us to establish it as a pretty good night in football's social calendar.

One year, I thought we had lost the FA Cup. Liverpool had won it, beating Sunderland in the 1992 final, and we had the trophy on display with all the others at the dinner. Des Kelly, then with *Today* as their man on Merseyside, had taken responsibility for the cup's safe return to Anfield the next morning and arranged for it to be put in his room overnight. As chairman, I got a frantic call about 9.30am to say the FA Cup had disappeared! Des claimed it had never been put in his room. After half an hour of panic, a second check revealed the cup was there after all. Des thought the wooden box the trophy was in was the mini-bar!

Lost the FA Cup? I once lost an entire banqueting suite and about 700 guests. I slipped out to relieve myself during a big sporting dinner in the Royal Lancaster Hotel, in London, and somehow took a few wrong turnings on the way back and found myself in a deserted suite. I was on the wrong floor. I was so disorientated, I had to pick up a house phone and ask for directions. Spooky.

I can also admit to emptying two banqueting suites, at the Midland Hotel, Manchester (now the Crowne Plaza Holiday Inn) and the Imperial Hotel, Blackpool. On each occasion I was at the microphone when the fire alarm went off and we had to leave the building.

A final word on awards dinners. Very embarrassing. I was chairing the Speedway Writers and Photographers Association awards dinner at that same Midland Hotel when the legendary

Jack Parker, a star before and after the Second World War, was guest of honour. He was to receive an inscribed silver tankard and just as one of our other guests got up to eulogise about Jack, I realised the tankard was missing.

I made frantic hand signals to our treasurer who was supposed to have brought the tankard and who was sitting at another table. I mouthed the words 'Where's Jack's tankard?' No response. In desperation I mimed someone picking up a tankard and drinking from it—and then pointed, as discreetly as possible, at Jack Parker. Our treasurer promptly called a waiter over and ordered Jack a pint of bitter!

Where a few journalists are gathered together you are likely to find a modicum of alcohol and very few abstainers. Funnily enough, I recall a sponsored buffet lunch some years ago when the majority of us kicked off with tonic water or orange juice. It was the press launch of one of my speedway books, published by Stanley Paul, and they obtained the backing of *Pernod*. So we all trooped into Salon Pernod in London's Bond Street only to discover it was a Pernod-only bar. I got some merciless stick for that from my Fleet Street colleagues and I don't like aniseed myself. But it's amazing how quickly you can develop a taste after a couple of glasses of water.

Castlemaine had a big promotion of their XXXX lager at an England-Australia Test series a few years back and one of the English press corps nearly started a fight at Headingley by suggesting the Aussies only called it XXXX because they couldn't spell 'PISS'!

A few years ago the British Indoor Ice Speedway International at Telford was sponsored by *Bonkers*, manufacturers of contraceptives. It made the publicity material a bit tricky and free samples are not a lot of use if you have had the 'snip'.

I have to say sports sponsors, in my experience, have tended to be very generous to the media and it's embarrassing to see the frantic scramble for 'freebies' as soon as someone takes the lid off an *Umbro* or an *Adidas* box. You get the impression that if they were giving away gas masks free, somebody would knock you over to get the first one.

Anyway, to *Carling, Cornhill Insurance* and all the companies who plough their money into sport, at every level ... where would we be without you? Sober, probably.

Seventeen

TABLOID SPEAK

THE simple fact is, nobody speaks the language of tabloid newspapers. Can you imagine having a conversation with your family over breakfast that goes anything like this:

HUSBAND: 'Is your mother coming over Sunday?'

WIFE: 'Do you mean Wigan's queen of sheen, 65-year-old peroxide blonde mother of ten, Nell Phipps? No, the glamorous gran is set for a block-busting bid to abseil from the top of Blackpool Tower.'

HUSBAND: 'Wowee! I guess fans from all over the north will pour into the poor man's Las Vegas and pack the prom from dawn to give the perky pensioner moral support.'

WIFE: 'And what are your plans for the day, luv?'

HUSBAND: 'I'm playing bowls with love-tangle vicar Harry Prendergast, 48, and 35-year-old Padiham tripe dealer Bert Higginbottom.'

WIFE: 'You'd better keep a tight rein on your temper because you've been walking a disciplinary tightrope since you plummeted down the Fair Play rankings after that ugly brawl with one-eyed car salesman Fred Scuttle, 36, from Colne.'

DAUGHTER (aged 17): 'Well, I'm about to flee our £60,000 red brick semi in tree-lined Acacia Avenue after stunning revelations about my two-year affair with serial arsonist Ivor Match, 34. I fear I'm doomed to a life in exile. But first I'll tearfully munch through

this bacon sandwich and sip my piping hot coffee.'
SON (acne-ridden and aged 8): 'I'm still recovering from being snatched from within inches of death after my four-hour ordeal trapped in a disused mineshaft. I owe my life to four-year-old Lucky, the tenacious terrier.'

Can you believe this shi-s-s-stuff? I bet you have read plenty like it. Why do tabloids seem to think we want to know the age of everybody from the Shah of Persia to the ship's cat? And what about the front page banner headline that reads 'M5 RAPE FIEND WAS MY LOVER, SAYS MODEL'. Can you imagine anyone actually saying something like that?

Impact and economy of words is the reason for short, sharp, dramatic headlines. If you are a sub editor on the *Sun* or the *Mirror*, working on a story about Argentina's footballers being involved in a brawl and the requirement is a two-line headline, no more than six letters in each line, you'd be hard-pressed to come up with something better than 'ARGY BARGY'.

Words of one syllable fit cosily into tabloid headlines. 'SOAP HUNK SLAMS RACE-HATE COPS,' a page lead in the *News of the World*, is a fairly typical example. That's why we launch 'probes' instead of 'investigations' and 'disciplinary measures' become 'raps'.

The popular tabloids may be regarded as 'comics' in some quarters, even as the 'gutter press' in others but they are masters at producing eye-catchingly humorous splash headlines. *The Sun* came up with 'DIDN'T WE DIDGERIDOO WELL' and 'ROOS AFRAID OF THE BIG CAD WOLF?' when our cricketers beat Australia in the First Test in 1997.

Down the years there have been some classic headlines, many of them a little risqué but nonetheless amusing. Classic examples: 'DR FUCHS OFF TO POLE AGAIN' ... '8th ARMY PUSH BOTTLES UP GERMAN REAR' ... 'COX AND DICKS OUT AT BRISTOL'.

Back in the 60's—when headlines were handset in type and not drawn up on a computer—the *Daily Mail* had a slogan which was printed on thousands of car stickers and posters and read The *Daily Mail* leads. Simple and effective. But one night, when I was the stone sub on sport, I had a mini-crisis right on edition time and had to change the splash headline because we had run out of L's! I told the marketing department they should change their slogan to The *Daily Mail* 'eads.

Much the same style and economy applies to tabloid writing. And it is amazing how we use words and phrases in copy that we would never think of using in conversation. Why do people in tabloid stories always seem to 'plummet' instead of 'fall', 'quaff' or 'sip' instead of 'drink', 'puff' instead of 'smoke' cigarettes and 'scoop' instead of 'win' pools or lottery jackpots?

Why do people take 'vows of silence' and doctors and nurses go on 'mercy dashes'? Why are errant schoolchildren and rebel sports stars given 'tongue lashings' or 'read the riot act'? How many times have you looked at the sports pages and read about a soccer manager who is 'set to plunge for out-of-contract Villa star' or 'faces the chop' or 'launched a bitter verbal attack' or worse?

In tabloid-speak a disagreement between two clubs or players is always 'a war of words'. Managers always seem to be 'swooping' or 'plunging' to 'splash' millions to 'launch a title bid'. They are forever 'jetting' out on 'top-secret spying missions' while players 'pledge' to do this, that and the other. In cricket we get 'a run blitz' or a 'wicket blitz', tennis players and athletes 'power' their way to victory. Football grounds become 'white-hot cauldrons' or 'pits of hate'. A few extra security measures become 'a ring of steel'. And so it goes on.

I've known some great guys who were masters at tabloid-speak. Arthur Brooks was one, in the days when *The Mirror's* northern production was housed in Withy Grove, Manchester. Like me, Arthur lived in a village at the foot of the Pennines and often suffered from the extremes of winter. He phoned the news desk one morning from home, when the north was in the grip of one of those unexpected, overnight blizzards and he was snowed in. 'We need a good line on this weather story, got any ideas?' he was asked.

'Sure,' said Arthur. 'Give me ten minutes and I'll be on to copy.' As promised, he filed a graphic account of 'The White Hell of Saddleworth' ... Pennine villages cut off, cars abandoned in ten-feet high drifts, power lines down, doctors and vets battling through blizzards to deliver babies or dig sheep out of the snow as the fury of winter took its toll on an innocent community. It was tear-jerking stuff. A few hours later, when the first northern editions were rolling and Arthur's gripping account was the splash ... in walked Arthur. The news editor looked up, startled. 'How the bloody hell did you get here?' 'On the bus,' said Arthur. 'It's thawing!'

Arthur was into ghosting footballer's autobiographies and agreed a deal to write the story of one of Bill Shankly's major signings, big Ron Yeats. Ron, who had begun his adult working life in a slaughterhouse, said 'I don't know where to start.' Arthur thought for a moment, clicked his fingers and said 'From the abattoirs of Aberdeen to the arc-lights of Anfield. Take it from there, kid.' He should have been in the movie classic Casablanca.

The old *Daily Sketch* used to have a Manchester soccer writer called Ken Ashton, who wrote some fairly over-the-top stuff. He once kicked off his Easter soccer preview with the following : 'Stand by for a spoonful of eggs-traordinary, eggs-certificate Bank Holiday title action. The north's top clubs are in for the biggest Easter crunch since Humpty Dumpty launched himself into the original omelette.'

Manchester was a thriving newspaper production centre until the *Sun* pulled out and, against nearly all the forecasts, not only survived but became the No 1 seller.

In the 80's more and more northern production journalists were made redundant or became almost totally dependent on head office when it came to decision-making. I did hear that when one northern-based sports sub-editor got married and the vicar asked 'Do you take Marcia Jane Whatever to be your lawful wedded wife?' he replied 'Just a minute ... I'd better check with London!'

Suddenly, like the 'inkies' and the linotype machines, they were gone, apart from the skeletal editorial staffs and the *Manchester Evening News*. No more hustle and bustle and chaos as edition time approached, no more shrieking at copy boys and sending them to the library or the canteen, often on futile missions.

One nervous, spotty-faced lad on his first day as a copy boy, soon sampled the news editor's temper at edition time, when he was despatched to the canteen to buy the chain-smoking ogre twenty Senior Service. He returned empty-handed. 'Sorry, sir, they've got no Senior Service', apologised the copy boy. 'Then go back and get me something else.' 'What, sir?' 'Anything, any-thing, any-bloody-thing,' screamed the news editor. This time the copy boy returned with a pork pie!

The pressure on tabloid sports writers to come up with exclusives, day after day, or in the case of the Sundays, week after week, is fairly horrendous. It's not enough to have an 'exclusive' any more. It has to be a 'world exclusive'—as if the rest of the world cares that player 'x' has signed a new boot deal or eats three Shredded Wheat for breakfast.

And there are those who are what might be termed 'economical with the truth'. But it is hardly surprising when the market place is rife with rumour and speculation. You can always 'harden up' a story by quoting 'a source close to the club' or 'an insider'. You can also be left with egg on your face, if someone gives you a bum steer or circumstances change ... as I was in suggesting Frank Clark would succeed Terry Venables as England coach. My office took a shine to that one, because the source of the information was reliable, 'hardened up' the story and got it wrong. I got it wrong. Some you win, some you lose.

Quotes, or 'nannies', are considered vital to tabloid stories. Match reports, even 'considered' pieces, rewrites, tend to be used as an inside spread with 'the quotes story' leading the back page. The more outrageous or controversial the better. Bland quotes soon become punchy. 'There's not much to say except that it was a typical 0-0 and the ref should have given us a couple of penalties' can easily become 'Fergie fury over Ref.'

The quicker you get some 'nannies' on to copy, the better the subs like it. And it's not easy if you are kept waiting for players and managers. Years ago, before you could pick up a quick after-match quote from radio or television, I heard another national paper reporter phoning his rewrite within minutes of the full-time whistle at a night game. It started off something like: Hat-trick hero Les Smith shot battling County into the fifth round for the first time for 20 years and bubbled "I'm over the moon. That's one of the best hat-tricks I've ever scored and I'll be sleeping with the match ball under my pillow tonight. But don't give all the credit to me … it was a team effort."

I looked at my fellow scribe in amazement and said 'How did you get those quotes? You've never been out of the press box and the game only finished ten minutes ago.' He just grinned and said 'I'm not waiting half an hour for him to say the same thing. He's not going to argue about any of that, is he?' Not much. The 'hat-trick hero' later admitted to the rest of us that he had only scored twice and wouldn't be claiming the match ball. What is it they say about cheats never prosper?

Gary Lineker, in his footballing days before he became a media man, said 'I didn't realise what the tabloids were like when I was younger and I was caught out. Now I never answer "Yes" or "No" to any question because if they ask you if you think England can beat Italy and you say "Yes", the headline will be "We'll beat Italy, says Lineker".'

Having said all that, the tabloids DO break most of the big stories because if you dig deep enough and often enough, you are going to come up with something better than a shovelful of manure.

The Mirror's award-winning Harry Harris churns out 'world exclusives' in his sleep, a prolific 'digger' and wordsmith with a contacts book some of us would kill for. The late Robert Maxwell, former MGN mogul and the pensioners' friend, rated Harry so highly he insisted he accept a brand new motor as a bonus. 'Don't want one, thanks,' said Harry. 'I insist,' boomed Captain Bob. 'Anything you like ... BMW, Merc, Audi.' 'I'm fine, I really don't want one.' Dictators don't listen to reasons, don't take 'No' for an answer, so Harry relented. The reason he didn't want a new car was because he didn't drive! True story? World exclusive? Who knows?

Harry does seem to be a 'whipping boy' for some of his contemporaries. He is alleged to be the author of such outrageous statements as 'From my hotel room overlooking Mount Everest' ... 'The bulldozers are hovering over Stamford Bridge' ... 'Bethlehem - birthplace of the legendary Jesus Christ.' Put it down to envy, Harry.

Tabloids, even middle-of-the-road ones like *The Express* and the *Daily Mail*, come up with gimmicks to try to boost circulation. A former editor of the *Sunday Express* decided to introduce 'celebrity reports' on top football matches, including the FA Cup Final. The idea may have been alright in theory because it brought the paper no end of free 'plugs' on radio and television. It was a bit of the old 'Ego has landed' again.

Where it was wrong, totally wrong, was that all the 'celebs' were fanatical supporters of one or other of the teams they were writing about. And they wrote, albeit humorously, about why they were fans, more than about the match. So how could the paper have any credibility reporting games like Manchester United v Arsenal or Spurs v Liverpool? It DID work when the celebrity report was used alongside a balanced piece.

I believe there was a major panic at the *S.EX.* on the first day of the new football season when the celebrity column was about to be introduced. A high-profile politician was lined up to do a Premiership game but his copy was late. No wonder. He phoned the sports editor's home by mistake. And what do we usually say to our wives when they call us at work when it's right on edition time?

Another longer-established gimmick in various tabloids is a Spot the Ball competition where, in case it has passed you by, you are shown an action photograph from a match, with the ball painted out. And you have to put your 'x' where you think the ball should be. There is a story that an Irish Sunday paper forgot to paint out the ball one week, yet 35 per cent of their readers still put the 'x' in the wrong place. They thought the round thing, above the players' heads, was the moon!

Keep taking the tabloids. You never know, they might do you some good.

Eighteen

ALL ABROAD

TRAVEL, they say, broadens the mind and I love it. Maybe I haven't been to half the places some of my contemporaries have, spending so much time in aeroplanes their wives give them boarding passes before they go upstairs to bed. But I have been fortunate enough to venture outside the front door once or twice and who knows what new horizons lie ahead.

This chapter is not about 'Trains, planes and automobiles' because we've done all that. It's about the places at the other end ... although I did omit to mention being BOOED onto a coach in Poland! My one and only 'day trip' behind the 'Iron Curtain', the one that ended up stuck all night on the runway in Krakow with the pilot from Wolverhampton, the duff electrics and the cold engines. Remember?

I tell you something. I could have been waiting a hell of a lot longer to get out of Poland. I spent so much time scurrying around the pits and the dressing rooms after that 1973 world speedway championship final, chasing stories and interviews for various provincial newspapers and radio stations, I forgot I had come on a supporters' trip. The coach taking us back to Krakow for the return flight was due to leave the Slaski Stadium in Katowice at 7.30pm on the dot.

When I remembered ... it was about twenty to eight and I still had three radio interviews to do, jobs that were helping to pay for the trip. So, naively, I took a decision to stay ... Sod the bus, the flight is not until midnight, it's only 100 kilometres to Krakow and I can bum a lift with one of the riders. Half-eight, job done, but a bit of a problem. No riders going anywhere near

Krakow. 'You'll have to go into Katowice and get a train', suggested one of the FIM officials, matter of factly.

So I put away my notebook, closed up the BBC Radio Manchester uwer (tape recorder) and headed for the exit. Now, any of you who have been to the Slaski Stadium will know that it is situated in the middle of acres of parkland surrounded by lakes and gardens. So when I hit the darkness, on my first-ever trip to Poland, I hadn't a clue which direction to go in to find Katowice. Only then, did it start to dawn on me I had no credit cards, very few Zlotys and couldn't speak a word of Polish.

A western journalist wandering unchaperoned in an Iron Curtain country. Not a good idea. I reflected on the trouble I had had getting a visa from the Polish consulate, an 11th hour scramble with someone from the *Daily Mirror's* London office chasing up the Polish Motor Federation after a number of rebuffs.

As I plodded wearily in the rough direction of the main road, one solitary coach stood dimly lit in one of the car parks. It looked strangely familiar. It couldn't be, not at this hour. But it was. I recognised the colour, then the number, then some of the faces at the window—angry ones. I climbed aboard, muttering my heartfelt apologies, and was roundly booed all the way to my seat. I didn't care ... I felt as though I'd won the pools.

I've been back to Poland many times, Warsaw, Wroclaw, Lodz, Poznan and four more times to Katowice. In fact, when Peter Collins won the 1976 world final there it was one of the most memorable days of my life as well as his. Gordon Burnett of the *Daily Express* christened me 'Zloty Botty' on that trip, because I was P.C.'s business manager. But there's not a lot you can buy with zlotys—even in Poland!

Seven years later, when the country was really oppressed, I had a grim trip to Lodz with Liverpool in the midst of winter. It was made more uncomfortable by the fact I had a quite serious and steadily worsening stomach condition, which necessitated extra trips to the toilet.

Liverpool's charter flight had a lucky escape landing in fog and snow at Warsaw and then we had a three-hour ride in a rickety old bus. When I made my problem known to the courier, he said we would be stopping halfway. We did ... in an isolated, snow-covered car park. The public toilets were closed so it was a case of squatting in the snow, in the dark, against a backdrop of fir trees and howling wolves. What a glamorous job this is, I thought.

I was even taken short during the game and had to leave the press box just before half-time. If you think Wembley is bad for toilets, try the LKS Stadium in Lodz. No paper, no lock and when I heard the half-time stampede coming and put my foot against the door, it opened OUTWARDS!

It's funny how you remember the bad trips, the cock-ups and the headaches before the ones when everything goes like clockwork, the weather is brilliant, the hotel superb, the hospitality first class, the match a thriller and the stories plentiful. Hairy flights, eleven-hour coach journeys, nightmare taxi rides with kamikazi roadhogs at the wheel, cross-channel ferry trips in a force eight gale, etc. They're the memories that come back to haunt you.

The *Sunday Express* sent me to the World Cup Finals in Spain in 1982 but only because I was so desperate to go I made a personal plea to the editor John Junor. And because I was an 'extra', as far as the budget was concerned—the paper was already sending the chief sports writer James Mossop and the chief Scottish sports writer Ken Robertson—I had to do it on the 'cheap'. That meant booking a 14-day self-catering 'holiday' in Benidorm to get the cheapest possible flight out of Manchester to Alicante.

The idea was to dispense with the accommodation bit, hire a car in Alicante and stay modestly at a hotel in Valencia, where Northern Ireland were based. I was happy enough with that apart from the flight to Alicante with a load of pissed-up lads from Accrington and Bolton who nearly had us all thrown off before we left Manchester.

The Irish were the makeweights along with Honduras in a group headed by Spain, the host nation, and strongly-fancied Yugoslavia. It turned into a fairy story, with Billy Bingham's boys surviving the heat, the humidity and Spain's thuggery in the final game, to win the group. What a bloody good story!! The only problem was, my Benidorm 'holiday' was up. I was due to return the car to Hertz at Alicante Airport the next day and fly home with the boys from Accrington, if they weren't locked up in some Spanish dungeon.

'You can't come home,' said my sports editor, the next morning. 'You've got to stay with Northern Ireland. They're big news NOW! You'll have to go on with them to Madrid.' 'But what about the hire car and the return flight?' 'That's not my problem ... you're on London's budget from now on. They'll have to wire you some more money.' Charming. Talk about passing the buck. Still, I thought, no more squid butties, I can have a decent meal now!

But the money didn't come through until the following Wednesday so I had to beg and borrow from the other press lads—and stick to the squid butties! I finished up, ten days later, paying nearly £300 scheduled air fare to get home from Madrid via Heathrow. So much for the 'false economy' of that cheap package holiday. Can you believe the skinflint management pen-pusher in the Manchester office seriously wanted to know if there was any way of getting a refund on the unused return flight from 'Benidorm'?

It was a great experience and the Irish lads were brilliant, on and off the pitch. And for those who think that all scribes are happy to dig the dirt, I can reveal that the 'Sunday' men 'sat on a story' that would have ruined their finest hour. The Friday night they beat Spain in Valencia a few drinks were sunk in celebration and the next morning, one of the players was sporting a black eye.

Investigations revealed that he had been 'winding up' another player on a personal matter and the joke had gone a bit too far. The other player had 'snapped' and landed him one. That was it. A one-punch argument. Nothing to do with the World Cup and no recriminations.

There was general agreement amongst the journos that we had more than enough strong copy about Spain's tactics (they were dubbed The Butchers of Valencia in the *News of the World*) and Ireland's glory and that if this particular story had been 'blown up' it would have distorted the real picture. Sadly, common sense would not prevail these days.

Here's something. I wonder how many people can claim to have watched a European Champions Cup semi-final seated on a park bench? Furthermore, reported on it from that same bench? It happened to me and a couple of the other Sunday lads in Switzerland, in April 1977, when Liverpool played FC Zurich. The press box was so full that some of us were allocated seats on a slatted, green park bench right behind one of the goals.

The pitch had an athletics track round it so we had acres of space. By co-incidence I had arranged to do my *Sunday Express* feature on Liverpool's England international goalkeeper Ray Clemence and that unexpected vantage point couldn't have been better. I could hear every curse he hurled at his defenders and his vitriolic reaction to being beaten from the penalty spot after only six minutes. Liverpool did go on to win 3-1.

'Clem' and Phil Neal were great mates yet the way they bawled each other out during that match made the exchanges Manchester United's Peter Schmeichel has with his defenders seem like whispered 'sweet nothings'.

English is so widely-spoken wherever you go in the world that very few of us make sufficient effort to learn more than the rudiments of another language. According to my pal Norman Wynne, now retired from the *Sunday People*, Horace Yates, of the *Liverpool Daily Post*, made a token gesture in restaurants by always ordering 'Oeuf and chips'.

How I envy the linguists amongst us who don't have to wait for the interpreter's quirky translation. What are you supposed to make of an after-match assessment like 'The ball is of the foot very good tonight and we are pleasing to make the play in the first half as many times we have it. Then it is close to make a draw. Thank you.'

We have been spoiled rotten by intelligent, worldly Europeans like Ruud Gullit, Jurgen Klinsmann, Johann Cruyff and Franz Beckenbauer. Twenty years ago I watched in awe in the press room at Barcelona's palatial Nou Camp Stadium as Cruyff politely, patiently and fluently answered questions in four different languages. And that was minutes after being knocked out of the UEFA Cup by Liverpool!

In contrast, when Liverpool lost a European Cup second round first leg in Helsinki some years later, puzzled Finnish journalists asked us 'Why is it Mr Paisley will not come to the press conference? We know Liverpool will win over the two legs but tonight is so important for Finnish football. We cannot understand his attitude.'

If that tie wasn't memorable for Liverpool diplomacy, it was for the performance of the Helsingin JK goalkeeper, Englishman Jeff Wood, on loan from Colchester United, who celebrated a famous victory by doing a solo lap of honour to the delight of the small crowd. Or so it seemed. As the Sunday papers were able to reveal 'exclusively' he actually ran round the track to give his car keys to his girl friend and simply acknowledged the cheers by waving back to the fans.

On my first-ever trip abroad, a camping holiday in Norway when I was in the sea scouts, I paid dearly for my ignorance of the language. I bought what I thought was the Norwegian equivalent of cola, took a swig and discovered it was malt vinegar. I should have learned my lesson then. Still gullible, I went to Germany to see a speedway meeting on a Sunday afternoon years later. Some friends, who collected programmes, asked me to buy them one if there were any. So I bought five and couldn't believe the price of them until I realised, too late, they included the admission fee.

The participation of English football clubs in European competitions, pioneered by Matt Busby and Manchester United in the 50's, did more than package holidays to change the eating habits of sports writers. Let's face it, the highlight of a working trip abroad is not the match but a good night out on the eve of it. I remember Kevin Keegan in Dresden when the press lads were waiting to 'hit the town'. He gave us all a withering look and said 'If I have another life I'm coming back as a football writer.'

When you think about it, sports stars go to some of the most exotic locations in the world and hardly see anything of them. Airports, hotel, training pitch, hotel, stadium, airport—particularly now football clubs and international squads only stop one night on most European trips. Then, if they do get a chance to go on the town themselves, one drink too many and they finish up on the front page of the tabloids. These days they can't even risk going to the dentist!!

Given the opportunity to see a little of some of the world's great cities, like Paris, Rome, New York, Rio, Prague, Moscow, Washington, Sydney and others, it always baffles me that one or two press men never leave the team hotel, except for the match and the trip home. I would rather go out into 'down town' Sofia or Poznan or Izmir and risk being mugged or having a bad meal, than settle for a night in the hotel with its international cuisine and over-priced bars.

Some press men don't have too much idea where they are going. When Ipswich flew to Germany on a European mission, the *Daily Mirror* man was heard to ask 'Is this Cologne gaff on the coast?'

There was a time when clubs stayed at least two nights on European trips and when the players were free to let their hair down after a match. I would argue they got on better with the media then than they do now. You should hear some of the tales my older colleagues tell of players and press in years gone by—but they would never dream of putting it into print.

I would be a liar if I tried to suggest press men never wandered into shady clubs or 'red light' areas for a bit of harmless fun. After all, if you're in Amsterdam, once you've seen one canal you've seen them all. A group of us were having a laugh and a drink in a bar in the notorious Kanalstrasse when a girl approached and asked if we would like to partake of her favours. One of the lads, who shall be nameless, said 'You're too pretty, luv. I want someone fat and wrinkled, with varicose veins, a hair net and a fag hanging out of her mouth.' The girl was amazed. 'Why is this?' she asked. 'Cos I'm bleedin' 'omesick, luv.'

I have it on good authority that one of the great old campaigners of the north east, Charlie Summerbell, decided to give his pals a treat and, at the same time, 'send up' the girls who pose in windows in 'red light' districts. He and his mate were walking some way ahead of their colleagues when Charlie nipped into one of the 'shops', paid the girl a few guilders to borrow her chair in the window, stripped down to his vest and underpants and took out his teeth. As his press pals continued their 'window shopping' expedition they were suddenly confronted by Charlie posing in all his glory.

There are clubs around the world where girls, with astonishing control of their vaginal muscles, can write you a short note with a felt-tip pen. A *Daily Star* reporter returned from a trip to Amsterdam to hand his sports editor a note which read 'From one **** to another'.

Practical jokes are rife among the press corps and the 'snappers' (photographers) played a corker on one of their own, affectionately nick-named 'Captain Pugwash', in Sardinia during the 1990 World Cup. He was fascinated that when the maids serviced his hotel room, they always placed a yellow paper flower petal on the water in the toilet. Every day without fail. He didn't speak the lingo so he couldn't find out why. Then one of the other 'snappers' told him there was a snake in the sewerage system and the petal was chemically-treated to keep it at bay. You can imagine the song and dance the frantic 'Captain Pugwash' made the next day when, surprise, surprise, there was no petal in his toilet. The staff at the Forte Village are still wondering what the hell he was raving about. 'Snake, signor? What snake?'

The 1990 World Cup Finals grew from little acorns as far as England were concerned. Few of us, or the people back home, gave them much of a shout after their sterile performance against the Republic of Ireland in their opening group game in Cagliari. They were at war with the media and detached from the real core of the tournament for too long in their Sardinian hideaway. But it got better, so much better, and by the time they faced the Germans in the semi-final in Turin they were on a roll.

And how well they played, denied a place in the final by the lottery of a penalty shoot-out—as were the hosts, Italy. If only the third-placed play-off I saw in Bari had been the final because Germany v Argentina in Rome stunk the place out.

Relations between the England party and the press improved with the performances and also after a behind-closed-doors clear-the-air session called by manager Bobby Robson in Bologna. A strong, intimidating police presence at training sessions had not helped the media's mood and when Robson asked for any general complaints by the press, one of our number got his wires crossed and chirped 'It doesn't help when we are being knocked about by the carbonaras!'

The magic of the World Cup attracts a media presence from far and wide and I chanced to meet up with the chief sports writer of *Penguin News*—the weekly newspaper of the Falkland Islands. Okay, so penguins can't read but when they outnumber the humans to such an extent you have to give them a little consideration. Patrick Watts travelled to Italy at his own expense to cover the finals on behalf of the 2,000 islanders and

2,000 British troops stationed there. Naturally, he was hoping for an England-Argentina final and he nearly got it.

Italia 90 was a six-week mini-marathon, including the acclimatisation period in Sardinia and a friendly in Tunisia. I would be a liar if I said it was ever anything less than enjoyable— apart from terrifying taxi rides from Naples down to Sorrento. The whole experience was very different from the usual hop into Europe with a club side.

The brief for 'daily' newspaper men on a midweek club trip into Europe is fairly straightforward. Preview, match report, follow-up. Anything else is a bonus. 'Sunday' men have to take a different tack, looking for the follow-up beyond the follow-up, trying to second-guess the 'dailies'. If my sports editor wanted an in-depth feature it was difficult to pick the right man BEFORE the game. What if he got injured or had a 'stinker'? The big bonus was a hard-news line for the back page and, in Liverpool's case, the club were so media-conscious they often provided the story on a plate.

The 'dailies' got their share but such was the rivalry, it did lead to a certain amount of animosity. Even our informant had to lay false trails before revealing the 'Sunday line'. Whispered messages like 'Don't come to my room, it's too obvious. I'll be in Jim's room in half an hour.'

You can go on some trips, particularly with England, when you chase about for hours after the match and come back with absolutely nothing, story-wise, panic on the flight all the way home and then drop on a back-page lead in a chance conversation at Baggage Reclaim. Not good for the ulcer when it's as tight as that. Another time you can get lucky and 'win the jackpot.'

I had just taken my seat with two 'Sunday' colleagues/ rivals for the flight to Paris and the 1981 European Cup Final. Liverpool v Real Madrid. Tuesday morning. Too early to start worrying about stories that might hold until Sunday. Enjoy the flight, have a night out in Paris, talk and listen, do a couple of features, go to the match and THEN panic. That was the usual drill. Not on this occasion.

The *Sunday People* man rubbed his hands, grinned and whispered 'Right lads. We're going to enjoy this trip because we've cracked it. Back page lead. Kosher. Guaranteed to hold until Sunday'. Apart from the fact there are no such guarantees, it was indeed a kosher story.

Ray Clemence had 'pulled' my rival at the airport and told him he had a story the Sundays could use because he didn't want it to break before he flew off to South America with the England squad on the Saturday. He said he was going to leave Liverpool in the summer because he wanted to jump before he was pushed—knowing the exciting Bruce Grobbelaar was catching the eye in the reserves. 'Clem' didn't want his transfer request to drop on Bob Paisley's desk until he was en route to South America. And, nudge, nudge, wink, wink, he was on his way to Spurs as well. But NO quotes.

So it had to be written in the 'I understand', 'I am led to believe' style many sports writers use to protect their sources. But it was a cracker and the 'dailies' didn't get a sniff of it. So, what with Liverpool winning in Paris and finding another story or two for Sunday, it was just about as good a working trip as you can get. And if you're wondering why the *Sunday People* man didn't keep the Ray Clemence story to himself it was because he was given it on the understanding it was for all of us. We would have all done the same. I think.

England trips are different because there is such a massive media presence. Even at Wembley it is a struggle to get a good line out of a midweek international that will 'hold'. At least the England managers of my experience, Bobby Robson, Graham Taylor and Terry Venables, gave the 'Sundays' a chance to ask their own questions at separate press conferences. You had to take pot luck with the players.

How we could learn from the Dutch. When they played in Euro 96 in England, you went to their hotel at a specified time and ALL the players sat at individual tables to be interviewed. Out of courtesy you had to tell the press officer which player(s) you wanted to interview and they were each given a list, so they knew who they were talking to. All very civilised.

Like a good dinner and a good bottle of wine. And I've shared a few of those with David Barnes, my regular drinking companion on so many trips abroad.

Although the press can be a bit cliquish on trips, the camaraderie is pretty good. But we do tend to ride roughshod over other people's problems. Sometimes we are bowled 'bouncers' by our sports editors like 'Ask Graeme Souness if he has ever smoked pot?' We had just arrived in Athens for an England game when *The Mirror's* Nigel Clarke, now with the *Daily Mail,* got a call from his office.

Nigel doubled as the tennis correspondent and a story had broken back home. He came into the England press conference looking a bit perplexed. 'Bjorn Borg's supposed to be having a nervous breakdown and I've got to do 1,500 words on other famous sports stars who have cracked up under pressure. And they want it in half an hour. Got any ideas lads, I'm a bit desperate.'

Some genuine head-scratching went on before another daily man said, poker-faced 'Heh, Nige, I can tell you why Bjorn Borg is having a nervous breakdown, if that'll help ... (pause for effect) ... He can't turn the lights out on his Volvo!'

Nineteen

ARE YOU SITTING COMFORTABLY?

PRESS boxes are a bit like hotel rooms, they come in all shapes, sizes and classifications. Large, medium, small, very small. Comfortable, uncomfortable, accessible, inaccessible, high, low, hot, cold, with or without a decent view, occasionally en suite, five star, one star and 'you must be joking if you think I'm staying here!'

There are standing-up press boxes, leaning-against-the-wall press boxes, sitting-on-the-steps press boxes and even non-press boxes ... like sitting on the bonnet of a tractor at a speedway meeting, standing on a milking stool, mingling with the hoolies on the terraces, craning your neck in a gangway, sitting in the dug-out, walking the course, cycling along the river-bank and, by far the most civilised, standing at the bar.

The best place to be to report motor racing or speedway is the 'pits'. That's where everything happens. But access is strictly limited at big international meetings. I was refused entry at a world championship speedway meeting in Germany because I had the wrong colour pass. So I got in via a frankfurter stall!

It was a scorching hot afternoon and I noticed there was a door open at each end of the frankfurter stall, one to serve the riders and mechanics. So I barged my way through while they were serving the bangers and sauerkraut.

Having started my football reporting career sitting on the trainer's bucket, at Station View, the home of Harrogate Railway Athletic, I suppose the most bizarre, in my experience, in terms of what was meant to be the official press seating area at an international sporting event, was that park bench in Zurich, referred to elsewhere. But a row of chairs on a coal lorry took some beating. That was on offer at a world championship speedway meeting in Fredericia, Denmark. Later, when Ole Olsen's custom-built speedway stadium opened at Vojens, we progressed to a standing-up press box which was at least under cover. And when you go to Vojens you need to be under cover.

You can get soaked in the best of places. My first experience of the Stadium of Light, in Lisbon, the celebrated home of Portuguese soccer giants Benfica, was a terrible let-down. The press overflow—not a bad word for it on that occasion—was a block of concrete terracing near the touchline and exposed to a cloudburst that lasted for most of the game. Four of us sat on newspapers, without an umbrella amongst us, while Liverpool splashed to a European Cup quarter final first leg win in March 1978. Notebooks turned to papier-mâché in seconds. We couldn't have got wetter if we had stood in the showers fully-clothed and the only saving grace was that we didn't fly home straight after the game.

On another visit to the Stadium of Light, access to the press box was via a rickety 100 feet of makeshift stairs and scaffolding at the back of the main terrace, something I suppose TV and radio commentators are used to on a regular basis. I was relieved to discover on my last trip, for the Republic of Ireland's European Championships qualifying game in November 1995, the stadium had been renovated and a splendid new press box built behind glass. Bloody good job, because it was persisting down just like in '78!

The Wembley press box has been up and down the twin-towered stand like a yo-yo over the years. When I first started going it was behind glass in the restaurant, then it went upstairs to where they now charge mega-money and call it the Olympic Gallery. Now it is superbly located behind the Royal Box and the VIP seats—but it's outside and you can't hear yourself think. At least you can't complain about any lack of atmosphere, either.

And full marks to Wembley press officer Martin Corrie for involving the Football Writers Association in discussions about the media facilities for the 'new' Wembley.

Now there is a man whose job includes the headache of forged tickets, year after year. The demand for FA Cup Final tickets is greater than ever, in spite of saturation coverage on television. So the FA and Wembley constantly seek to make the tickets more and more sophisticated, like bank notes.

The trouble is, the forgeries become more sophisticated, too. Martin told me a great story about a recent forgery, for one of Manchester United's appearances in the Cup Final, that was so good the only giveaway was in the small print on the back which gives the 'terms and conditions' of sale.

'You needed a magnifying glass,' said Martin, 'to see that the forger had added the words "F*** off, you southern bastards!" Otherwise, we might never have known it was counterfeit.'

Clubs face huge problems when they play host to European games or international fixtures. Manchester United, Liverpool and Leeds were just three of the English clubs that had to build elaborate temporary media facilities on the opposite side of their stadiums to their normal press areas, for Euro 96; seats and desks for hundreds of journalists as well as providing a media lounge and working areas for day-to-day use and mixed zones for after-match interviews. UEFA and the FA took on extra staff and although there were the inevitable complaints about confusion and chaos on match days, it worked pretty well.

Normally, the clubs can cope with an overflow section for their own European club matches although when Liverpool were such a force in the 70's and early 80's, they simply didn't have the space to provide proper interview facilities or refreshments.

Everyone squeezed into the tiny press room at Anfield at half-time for a cup of tea and a biscuit, if you could get near the urn. 'With or without,' shouted the press steward, repetitively, like a newsvendor, offering cartons of tea 'with or without' sugar. It was hardly a phrase familiar to our European chums and I recall vividly a German reporter turning to me amid the mass of struggling humanity in the Anfield press room and asking, incredulously 'Vot iz dis vith or vithout, please?'

For several years now Liverpool have had a new, far more spacious press room, no shortage of refreshments and the unobstructed view from the press box remains as good as any in the country. Arsenal, Manchester United and Blackburn are among the clubs who have media interview theatres as well as press boxes and press lounges and new stadiums are, generally, providing the media with better facilities to keep pace with progress. After all, this is the age of the lap-top rather than the typewriter and electricity sockets are almost as vital as telephone points.

Yet some clubs still build press boxes as if they were designed for pygmies or seven-stone weaklings with postage-stamp sized lap-tops who are expected to retain liquid like ships of the desert. Once you are in, you are in to stay and often until beyond the half-time or full-time whistle. If you cop for a local radio guy sitting in the seat nearest the gangway, the chances are he is just about to go on air when everyone else is heading for the toilets and the half-time tea.

One of the problems over the last decade has been the local radio and Club Call 'explosion' and the fact that many clubs have accommodated their increasing numbers in boxes built originally just for the written press. A new radio station seems to hit the airwaves every week and they turn up in droves, with their ex-player summarisers and even their producers, and bring suit-cases full of equipment with them.

Nothing personal, lads and lasses, because I have done my share of radio work but it's a bit much when bone fide writers turn up for a big FA Cup tie, representing a national newspaper, and are squeezed out of the press box by a dozen 'lollipop men.'

When I covered York City v Liverpool in the FA Cup a

few years ago, not one seat in the press box was allocated to a Sunday newspaper. We had to sit on the touchline unless we could persuade one of our daily 'brothers' to do a swap. And then we had to move because we were obliterating one of the advertising hoardings.

We all appreciate the logistical problems involved in staging a big match on a small ground but why do the press have to get the short straw so often? I'll quote you two more examples from the FA Cup. Notts County v Everton, sixth round, 1984. I was there a good hour and a half before the kick-off because games like that may be romantic, they also spell 'trouble'. The enclosed press box in the old main stand at Meadow Lane was empty save for a steward who had at least done the decent thing and, like me, turned up early. He had a clipboard and a list of names, I showed him my pass, which had no seat number, and he duly ticked my name on his list.

I looked at the list, looked at the press box and did a quick count-up. I can't remember exactly but the number of seats in the box was about 18 and the number of names on his list nearer 30. 'How do you expect to get all those people into that box?' I asked. 'Are you trying to get into the *Guinness Book of Records*? Or are you going to stack them up or have two sittings?' 'No bloody idea, mate. It's not my problem.' 'Well, it's going to be when they all get here ... what are you going to do when the box is full. Where is the overflow press box?' 'There isn't one, mate. And they can't sit on the steps because that would constitute a fire hazard.' 'But suffocation is alright?'

Then there was Swansea City v Liverpool in January 1990 and another case of trying to squeeze a quart into a pint pot. Another early arrival, just in case, even though my ticket had a row and seat number. I checked in an hour before kick off, sat in my allocated seat at the end of the second row and took in the view of the Vetch Field. HALF the pitch! Absolutely sod all to the right of the halfway line. Why? Because they had partitioned off half of the press box so it could be used as a police security camera station. Bloody good job it was a 0-0 draw!

You can guarantee that on occasions like that and just when everyone has been more or less shoe-horned into a seat, some pillock will turn up two minutes after the kick-off and say 'Sorry chaps, train was late. Look, I've got a phone booked for the *Sunday Times* so I need to be seated somewhere adjacent. Thousand words runner and all that.'

Before mobile phones, the local corr was expected to provide a phone on the whistle for everybody. 'Er, have you ordered a phone? No, well if you don't mind sharing with *The Evening Advertiser, Evening Gazette, The People, Sunday Mirror, Sunday Express, News of the World, Observer, World of Sport, Grandstand* and *PA* ... then it's not a problem.'

Personally, I've lost count of the number of times I have been promised: 'You'll be okay because the guy from the *Pink* will be finished right on the whistle and I've only got a score flash after that.' Twenty minutes after full-time you are trying to prise the receiver out of his hand.

Some press boxes are so high up they give you a nose bleed or vertigo or both. When you take your seat at Barcelona's magnificent Nou Camp Stadium you could be watching ant-racing, the players look so minute. And if it's not the seat, then the access can be pretty unnerving. Cricket writers of my generation and older will recall the long, slippery steps up to the roof at Old Trafford before they first built a new, enclosed staircase and then re-sited the box on the other side of the pavilion.

It was a long trek up to the rooftop Press Box at Hampden Park and it was so old and rickety I was convinced it would fall off every time Scotland scored a goal. Thankfully, that wasn't very often, in my experience! The pavilion balcony at Aigburth was a bit like that, the cricket ground in Liverpool where you suspected a good six-hit would deposit the ball in the Mersey.

Some smaller football club grounds used to have press

boxes erected on stilts. Shrewsbury and Rotherham are two that spring to mind. I was at Shrewsbury's Gay Meadow in 1961 the night Walsall clinched promotion to the Second Division and some of their jubilant fans thought it would be a nice idea if they shook the press box off its stanchions. If that was today I'm sure a few managers would be helping them!

A rare visit to Aldershot in 1964 stokes up the memory of dropping a pencil through a gap in the floorboards and fully ten seconds later hearing a splash. Could it have been a delusion or were we sited over a well? If you sat in the old box at Preston North End's Deepdale, you could often see 30 or 40 players, two pitches and two footballs. The box was situated at the extreme right of the main stand and when you looked through the glass sides everything appeared in duplicate. It was probably okay in the fifties when you could see two Tom Finneys for the price of one!

The 'pigeon loft' at Ewood Park was another box we were happy to bid farewell. In the old days pipe smoke and condensation often reduced visibility to nil, occasionally to the relief of the inhabitants. In modern times an alternative obstruction was the radio and television equipment in the adjoining booth, if you were trapped in the most distant corner of the second row. And who was the bright spark who did away with the gents toilets at the Darwen end of the Nuttall Street stand?

We have to squeeze into a similarly uncomfortable 'shed' at The Dell and trust that when the Saints do move into a new home they will give us a sporting chance of escape in the event of a fire. You couldn't swing a cat in most press boxes and Oldham's is one of the oldest. But it's worth going just to see if anyone, apart from the locals, can open the coffee pot at half-time.

Manchester City's press box used to be one of the best, right behind the Directors' Box with a cracking view and an opportunity to pick up snippets of interest from visiting scouts and managers as well as directors of both clubs. Then City decided that prime spot was a potential profit-maker and moved us into three 'shoe boxes' at the back of the stand.

A lift is a bonus, especially for arthritis sufferers, but they used to have one at Everton that was slower than any defender. You needed to be there on a Friday to be sure of making Saturday's kick-off. And I think the one at Middlesbrough only goes twice a week. At the end of the day, it is the prerogative of the clubs to site us anywhere they like in their grounds but the argument that the press should have to pay for the privilege doesn't hold water. In simplistic terms, all it amounts to really is a free seat for a free advert!

Earlier in this chapter I mentioned buckets, park benches and coal lorries in the context of bizarre press facilities. Two lads who regularly cover Plymouth Argyle can beat that. When they, or their newspapers, were barred from Home Park, by Argyle chairman Dan McCauley, they used a crane and hoist outside the ground to lift them to a rather precarious vantage point above the roof of the stand. Ingenuity or madness, I'm not sure which.

One last football Press Box story for you and there is every chance it is apocryphal. It is about the *Manchester Evening News* reporter who took a homing pigeon to a derby match at Maine Road because there was a telephone strike. Someone had had the ingenious idea of using a pigeon to speed the final score back to the old offices of the MEN in Cross Street.

The 'running report' would be rushed to the office by motor cycle dispatch riders and the pigeon used only at the final whistle. City scored in the final seconds to snatch victory and our man, barely able to contain his joy and traditional Blue bias, scribbled the result on a piece of paper, attached it to the ring on the pigeon's leg and sent the bird soaring skywards from the Press Box.

Imagine his horror when he realised, too late, that the goal had been disallowed! He was last seen running across the forecourt at Maine Road shouting hysterically 'come back, come back'!

Twenty

NEVER WORK WITH CHILDREN
OR ANIMALS

ISN'T that what they say in show business? Well, the same could be said for sports writing. As a father of five and the reluctant guardian of a lop-eared rabbit, I have my share of paternal instincts but when they get in the way of a story I tend to side with King Herod.

Totally the wrong attitude, I agree, and I have been getting it wrong in that respect for far too long. Particularly when a child's logic can provide a better, quicker solution than a fuddled mind. Wasn't it a child who came up with the solution when a lorry was jammed under a low bridge and the adults involved were desperately chiselling at the brickwork and considering an alternative route? The child suggested 'Let the tyres down!' And the lorry passed under the bridge.

Many a time I could do with that kind of inspiration in the press box when the mind goes blank as deadline approaches. But there have been occasions when children and animals have been a hindrance and, in some cases, literally a pain in the backside.

I watched Nicky Summerbee flitting down the wing for Manchester City, before his move to Sunderland, and thought back to the day I tried to interview his famous dad, Mike, over lunch in one of the city's Italian restaurants. We've all had it. School holidays, mum working, got to 'mind the child'. And Mike DID apologise for bringing along Nicky, who was then about three, to the lunch.

On reflection, McDonalds would have been a far wiser choice of venue than the Isola Bella. But the die was cast and my only concern was getting Mike to give me some juicy stuff about why life had gone sour for him at Maine Road and he had joined Burnley. Unfortunately, young children get bored very easily when asked to sit quietly and Nicky was the norm. No, he was worse than that. On reflection, he was an INFANT terrorist!!

It was not a good idea to let him have a bowl of minestrone soup—and a large spoon. The larger the spoon, the better the effect when it is brought down flatly and heavily into the soup, a bit like dropping a brick into a bucket of water! Mike said 'Sorry' and 'Don't do that Nicky' and the waiter grinned through his teeth and said 'It's not a problem, sir'. As he did a few minutes later when Nicky blew down the straw into his full glass of Coca-Cola.

Nicky's other successful attempts to attract his father's attention included crawling under tables while I failed miserably to stamp on his fingers. What I had to admire was the boy's impeccable timing, each interruption coming just as Mike was about to answer a loaded question. It was a classic piece of sabotage.

Years later I was in the Spanish city of Pamplona to interview the former Liverpool favourites Sammy Lee and Michael Robinson, who were both playing for Osasuna. Michael, now a top sports presenter in Spanish television, came round to Sammy's apartment to do the interview and had his young son in tow—another 'terrorist', with a penchant for destroying cream cakes and using the butt of a toy pistol to test the resistance of some rather fine stained-glass doors.

On other occasions, I have visited footballers and cricketers at their homes when they have been 'minding the child(ren)' and struggled gamely to conduct an interview in the face of a hail of missiles, an invitation to fix a broken doll or play Buckaroo or, more often than not, howling and bawling. I have fed babies, even changed nappies in the pursuit of a story. But I draw the line at doing the ironing.

Many more interviews, conducted over the telephone, have been cut short by the sound of breaking glass or the equivalent of blue murder at St Trinian's. 'Have to call you back, mate, the baby's just stabbed the dog!'

But that's real life, isn't it? If it's any consolation to the aforementioned, children and parents, I was a 22 carat gold brat who wrecked everything that wasn't nailed down and would have loved to be set loose on an unsuspecting journalist or broadcaster.

Tom Tyrrell, of Manchester's *Piccadilly Radio*, was waiting outside the players' lounge at Old Trafford after a game, to snatch an interview with United's Northern Ireland international Sammy McIlroy, who had been the match-winner. Sammy came out with his young son, Sammy Junior, and Tom had a flash of inspiration.

Morecambe and Wise were in their hey-day and Tom asked Sammy Snr if his son knew the TV comedy duo's famous catch-phrase when one asks 'What do you think of it so far?' and the other replies 'Rubbish!'. 'Of course he does' said Sam, So Tom explained to the boy that he was going to interview his dad, about the match, and then bring in little Sam for the punch-line.

I was one of the 'Sunday' men waiting patiently for a few words with the match-winner and we watched fascinated as Tom set up his gimmicky interview. He waited for the cue from the studio, to go live on air, and launched into the interview. Eventually, Tom chirped 'We've also got Sammy Junior here today and I know he's a great fan of Morecambe and Wise. So what do you think of it so far, little Sammy?' 'CRAP,' said the boy.

My speedway promoter pal Ian Thomas's son Lyndon, who is now an airline steward, was still in short pants when he and his mother, Dorothy, were offered a lift home from a meeting while Ian was detained on business. The offer was made by an executive of Lada cars, who sponsored Hull and Newcastle, and duly accepted. Ian and some of his riders had use of Lada cars as part of the deal, an arrangement suddenly threatened when Lyndon piped up from the back seat 'Dad thinks Lada cars are crap, doesn't he mum?' Followed, almost immediately, by 'Why are you hitting me, mum?'

If it's not kids, it's animals. Dogs, cats, rabbits, hamsters, ferrets, guinea pigs, horses, snakes. Dogs, mainly. Why do so many sports stars have BIG dogs? Alsatians, Rottweilers, Doberman Pinchers, German wolfhounds, Labradors, Boxers, Pit Bulls. 'Don't worry, mate, he's just a big baby ... only bites people he doesn't like!' It's not much consolation if they like you because they slobber all over you, sniff your crotch, chew your notebook or moult all over your suit. And when they don't like you ... .

I had a painful experience covering a British Speedway Championship Final at Coventry in the days before mobile phones. Under pressure from the media, after years of fighting over two phone lines, the organisers arranged for some of us to pay a hire fee to local householders for use of their private phones after the meeting. I duly rang the bell of my designated house and was midway through a live broadcast, to *BBC Radio Manchester*, when the family's pet Alsatian escaped from the kitchen and started nibbling my buttocks.

When Graeme Souness quit as manager of Liverpool, in January 1994, I was one of the press corps despatched to stake out his luxurious home in Mere, Cheshire. When we got there, his two Rottweilers were prowling the drive behind the big wrought-iron gates and looked as if they hadn't been fed for a fortnight. If he had been there and opened the gates, none of us would have had the bottle to enter, short of wearing chain-mail.

I get on pretty well with 'Souey' and a month or two later, when he was still out of football, he did invite me in for a chat —but it took me a long time to get out of the car! And I thought it was a bit perverse of him to have coffee in the back garden while the dogs were rampaging. My fault, I'm just a coward. I've been nipped enough times in the line of duty, thank you.

One footballer of my acquaintance was Dr Doolittle and James Herriot rolled into one. David Harvey, the former Leeds and Scotland goalkeeper, is now farming somewhere in the Orkneys. I met up with him a few times in his days at Leeds and once spent a smashing afternoon with him in the market town of Driffield in the Yorkshire wolds.

He used to milk a Jersey cow called 'Goldie' before he set off for Elland Road. If he wanted a plumbing job doing he paid in kind 'A dozen eggs and a couple of chickens, that type of thing'. It was like a scene from *The Good Life*.

Animals have their place and my wife still hasn't forgiven me for taking her for a night out to a trotting track. Nice idea. A sub-editor pal invited us to go to this new night club-restaurant overlooking the track and have a meal and a bet. Neither of us had ever seen trotting, except on television, and it was a chance to put on the best bib and tucker. Great ... until our host insisted on taking us on a tour of the stables first. No wonder the head waiter screwed up his face and showed us to a corner table!

Twenty one

... AND THE NEXT PROGRAMME

FOOTBALL match programmes are team sheets that have turned into glossy brochures as thick as telephone directories and pricy with it. 'Couple of FA Cup Final programmes for the kids, sir? And one for yourself? Certainly. That will be eighteen quid! Oh, and perhaps you'd like to buy a suitcase to carry them in.'

Well, they don't exactly slip neatly into your inside jacket pocket the way programmes used to, do they? Foolscap size, as many as 116 pages. But you've got to admit they are high-class products and the quality and content of 'match-day magazines', as some like to call them, has improved immeasurably in the last decade.

Many clubs abroad still don't have programmes. They just flash the teams and adverts and any relevant information on to their electronic scoreboards. It doesn't seem right, does it? No programme, I mean. We are a nation of programme-lovers, even if we buy them and don't read them.

And it's bizarre that in this day and age we can charge as much as six quid—Chelsea v Middlesbrough, FA Cup Final 1997—for something that rarely fulfils its basic function, which is to tell you who is playing. We still have to look at the electric scoreboard or the team sheet or listen to the tannoy for that.

One way or another I have been involved in programme production for thirty-odd years, football and speedway in the main, writing columns, ghosting managers', players' and promoters' pieces; even down to designing and editing the whole shebang, as I still do for the British Indoor Ice

Speedway Championship at Telford every year.

I did five for Wembley, funnily enough. Not for the Cup Final. Out of my league. Indoor speedway at Wembley Arena, sponsored by Lada Cars. You have probably heard all the jokes about Lada cars but here's one with a punchline you wouldn't expect. They are more reliable than some of my programmes!

I dropped the mother and father of a clanger in my first Wembley programme. Almost literally, you could say, because I credited six times world speedway champion Ivan Mauger with an extra daughter. I even named her in the potty potted biography I wrote about him for that pioneering event in December 1979.

'Who is Vickie?' asked Ivan's wife Raye, with commendable restraint, at the after-meeting reception. 'We've only got three children. Your column in the programme says we've got four ... Julie, Debbie, Kym and Vickie. How long have you known us?' Fourteen years, actually. How do you explain a ricket like that to your own wife, never mind the wife of your star rider and co-promoter who both came to your own wedding?

And it wasn't the name of an old girl friend. In fact, to this day I've never been able to come up with a satisfactory explanation for that mental aberration other than that, for some reason, I had been under the impression the Maugers had three daughters, I was always vague on family matters and I had been over-working. It's frightening when a tired mind starts playing tricks as I know from a previous experience.

Ask anyone who produces programmes on a regular basis what a chore it can be trying to meet deadlines, churning out column after column, many off the top of your head and frequently in the early hours of the morning. When I was writing and producing the Hull speedway programme in the 70's and generally taking on too much with all my football work, I used to be lost in a fog of fatigue some nights. Even fell asleep over the typewriter. And because of the volume of copy, the time factor and printers based miles away, there was never any chance to see page proofs. Write 'em, print 'em, deliver 'em and sell 'em.

One race-day, when I wasn't able to get over to Hull for the regular Wednesday-night home meeting, the promoter rang me and said 'I've been having a look through tonight's programme and the printers have dropped a right bollock. They've got an action picture of one of last week's races and the caption says "Hull Lada Vikings star Bobby Beaton tries to overtake Bob Paisley and Bill Shankly!" 'What are you bloody talking about?' I said. I thought it was a typical Ian Thomas wind-up. 'No, I'm serious. That's what it says. Bit of a cock-up isn't it?'

I rang off, dazed, and immediately called up the printers in Leeds. 'Have you got the original copy for tonight's Hull programme? Good. Do you mind reading me the caption I wrote for the action picture on page seven. (Pause, while he found it and read it back to me) Jeeeesssus wept!!'

In moments of crisis, it is easy to look for scapegoats. I went on the attack, frenziedly. 'Well why didn't you change it? You must have bloody realised it was a mistake.' 'Listen, mate, you write the stuff, we print it. Ours is not to reason why.' 'So, I suppose if I wrote shit, you'd print it.' 'Well don't you?' Touché.

I was numb. I remember going outside, where my wife was sprawled out in a deck-chair in the afternoon sunshine, and saying to her 'That's it! I've flipped. I've gone bananas ... ' And when I told her why, she agreed. But wires do get crossed, brains do hoist the white flag occasionally and if you don't recognise the warning signs, you pay the price.

My wife Sue has often accused me of being a workaholic. A 'Sunday' man? Are you serious? She did remind me that in the first year we were married, I took on so much work that I was never away from the typewriter and forever demanding coffee. One day, to teach me a lesson, she put a tablespoonful of salt in my cup and I threw up over the Hull programme. I suppose most people did.

Back to the 'Paisley and Shankly' affair. Apart from the shock to the system, there was the fear of the repercussions. Not the 'sack' because the promoter was a good mate and also had bigger things to worry about. No, my nightmare was how the Hull fans would react, the letters, the humiliation. After all, I got a massive postbag of seven or eight letters a week for my regular 'Agony Aunt' column in the programme. Not one, not one letter, not even one cheap jibe when I dragged myself to Humberside the following week to face the music. I don't know what hurt most, the embarrassment of the gaff or the wounded ego because nobody noticed it.

But since I wasn't about to take the track microphone and ask the Hull fans what they thought of Bob Paisley and Bill Shankly riding round The Boulevard, I had to acknowledge the terrible truth that they only bought the programme to mark the score-card!

In my defence, I have written and produced scores of programmes and brochures for ice speedway internationals, testimonials, farewell meetings, golden jubilees, football, stock cars etc, without too many blips although when you've scored two 'own goals' like mine, you are lucky to stay on the pitch!

And talking of pitches ... I played for the Speedway Writers against the Speedway Riders in a charity football match at Port Vale when I was still fit enough to pull on a pair of boots. I was just settling into my creative, ball-playing, midfield general role when somebody kicked me about two feet in the air. As I picked myself up, an American international rider called Steve Gresham shouted 'That's for what you wrote about me in the Hull programme last season, you bastard!'

For a number of years now I have been contributing to the Leeds United and Manchester City programmes, a small cog in the Polar Print Group machine which has been consistently producing award-winning programmes. The fact that the Leeds and City programmes were voted the best in the Premier League and First Division, respectively, last season, in spite of my efforts, went some way to cleansing my conscience.

I had some fun doing the Rochdale FC programme in the early 70's. All of it ... for eight quid. I was free-lancing and told them their programme was a 'joke' and needed revamping. Not difficult when it carried league tables a month out of date, pen pictures of visiting players who had been transferred months before, a manager's column that always began 'I would like to extend a big welcome to the players and officials of' and always ended with 'so all I ask is that you get behind the lads.'

Another embarrassment was the number of mistakes in 'Today's Teams', which were either printing errors or down to the printer not hearing properly when the club phoned him the visitors' provisional line-up. If they didn't play for the Dale, he hadn't heard of them. For instance, had they been playing Manchester United in the FA Cup you would probably see something like 'Alick Stepney ... Tim Holton ... Fred McDougall ... Win Davies.'

One of the problems was dealing with a printer who had a heart of gold and was a loyal fan but saw no need for up-to-date league tables or revised biographies or manager's columns which actually included comments on the last game. It became a constant battle to break down the old barriers.

So where did the fun come in? In different ways. Along with many other programmes, we carried a player feature 'Personal Choice', fairly bland, repetitive stuff. The average poorly-paid Rochdale player of the period would say, for example, Favourite meal: Steak and chips. Favourite drink: Lager. Favourite holiday resort: Benidorm. Favourite car: Ford Cortina. Favourite TV programme: Match of the Day. Favourite film stars: Paul Newman and Sophia Loren.

Then one week my subject was a bit of a wag, a free-transfer signing from Hartlepool who was probably on about £50 a week. He sat there, poker-faced and listed the following: Favourite meal: Coq au vin served with basmati rice and ratatouille. Favourite drink: Harvey Wallbanger. Favourite holiday resort: St Lucia, Windward Islands. Favourite car: Lambourghini. Favourite TV programme: Open University. Favourite film stars: Rudolph Valentino and Mary Pickford. Well, at least he was different.

The apathy towards the football club was such that it was like pushing snow uphill to stoke up some interest. Fred Ratcliffe, the chairman, agreed to let me introduce a 'Rochdale Player of the Year' award and for five consecutive home games we advertised the fact in the programme, asked the fans to send in their postcard votes and offered a Main Stand Season ticket for the following season to the first name picked out of the hat. After those five home games we had the grand total of 21 votes. 'It's embarrassing', said the chairman. 'Wish we'd never agreed to it. How can you announce that the winner has only got 11 votes?' 'Simple. We just say he polled 52 per cent of the total vote.' 'R-i-g-h-t,' said Fred, which sounded like the cue for a song!

Anyway, Rochdale's fair-haired young striker Tony Buck was duly elected the club's Player of the Year and someone from Milnrow won himself a season ticket and promptly switched his allegiance to Bury! The following year, to get a more authentic result, we again advertised the competition in the programme but this time said we would ballot the fans at the penultimate home game. All they had to do was fill in a piece of paper as they entered through the turnstiles and drop it in a bucket. I'm happy to say it was a reasonably successful exercise. Out of a crowd 1,368 we received 447 votes although I have to admit three were for the tea-lady, two for the chairman, five for Donald Duck and one each for Cyril Smith MP and the late Gracie Fields.

Long after I moved on to other things, the team line-ups in the Rochdale programme could usually guarantee a chuckle. Two classics. They tried to turn George Oghani into an Irishman by putting an apostrophe after the 'O'. And, presumably, Brendan O'Connell must have had a sex-change operation to be listed as 'Brenda'!

Writing programmes is one thing, getting hold of one can be quite another. We have all experienced the frustration of getting to the ground late and finding that all the programmes have been sold. Have you noticed that it just makes you want one even more and you start blasting the programme sellers and stewards and demanding a reprint in the next five minutes. But what about the frustration for the club, having reduced the order after weeks of being left with boxes full of unsold copies.

My golden moment, in terms of frustration, was way back in the 60's when I travelled with Wolves to cover a First Division game at Fulham for the *Birmingham Sports Argus*. Because I was allowed on the team coach, I arrived at Craven Cottage a good hour and half before the kick-off and went into the ground through the 'Players and Officials' door. I pottered about in the press room for half an hour until the steward arrived and asked him for a programme. 'They've got them on the press entrance,' he said.

So I walked back through the main stand and somebody pointed me towards a 'jobsworth' standing at the press entrance. 'Can I have a programme, please?'

'Who are you, then?' 'Richard Bott, *Birmingham Sports Argus and Evening Despatch*' . 'How'd you get in? You didn't cum through this door. I 'avent ticked you off on my clipboard.'

'No,' I explained. 'I came on the team bus, early, and this door wasn't open. All I want is a programme.' 'Well, you'll have to go to the Secretary's Office now.' Which I did, only to be told 'These are all for the Directors and Guests. You get yours from the Press Steward.' 'Can I buy one?' 'Not inside the ground you can't.'

Back I went to 'jobsworth', thoroughly pissed off by now. But the fun was only just beginning, for him. 'They told me in the Secretary's Office I have to get a programme from you, because I'm Press.' 'Well, you aint getting one because you didn't come in through this door.' 'Right' I said, trying hard to keep my temper. 'I tell you what ... close your eyes while I go out into the street, walk up and down for a few minutes, come back and show you my press ticket. Then can I have a programme?'

That was a difficult one for 'Jobsworth' to handle. Like a MENSA test. He pondered for a while, rubbed his nose then remembered the golden rule of being a 'jobsworth' ... use the morsal of power you have been fed to be as bloody-minded and obstructive as possible ... at all times.

He stood erect, straightened his cap, looked dead ahead and said 'Nah. I'd know ... wouldn't I?' Bastard! As my old mate Don Evans used to say 'No wonder Hitler never invaded England. He wouldn't have got past the commissionaires!'

They are either intent on stopping you from coming in or throwing you out. The Wembley dressing rooms are either side of the famous tunnel and the team coaches park there. For years, until the FA made some effort to create a 'mixed zone' for interviews, those of us doing the 'quotes' were involved in some unseemly scuffles outside those dressing rooms, tripping over TV cables, being jostled by stewards, just to get near the players.

Often it was hard enough to get down to the tunnel in the first place, if either of the managers had requested 'No media access.' If you were a radio man with a lollipop (microphone) in your hand, it was open sesame. If you tipped the steward a few quid at the top of the stairs, you could sneak down a bit earlier than the rest.

After one particular League Cup Final, when Nottingham Forest beat Luton Town, the order was given to keep the press out of the tunnel. But I saw one of my 'Sunday' rivals 'bribe' his way down and had to do the same to make sure he didn't get an exclusive. Once down there, I found my rival standing outside the door of the Forest dressing-room with two radio men and a TV cameraman.

A po-faced steward approached at speed. 'Heh, you press ... OUT!' My rival said, coolly 'I'm doing a column with Mr Clough. I have his permission to be here.' It was all bollocks, of course. Cloughie wouldn't have given him the time of day. But 'jobsworth' bought it. 'Okay, you can stay but YOU (he pointed a nicotine-stained finger at me) ... OUT.' I protested that I had as much right to be there as the other guy but he wasn't having any and turned to a burly police constable who was on guard by the huge double doors that led out into the Wembley car park.

'Officer, I want this man thrown out now. He's press and he shouldn't be down 'ere', demanded 'jobsworth'. Brilliant, I thought, I'm going to be slung out into the crowd before I've got a single quote and my deadline is in ten minutes. But the policeman, bless his heart, just looked 'jobsworth' up and down, winked at me and said 'F*** all to do with me, mate!' And from that moment, 'jobsworth' bottled it.

The last word on 'jobsworths' goes to the doyen, Don Evans. An officious steward treated the English press corps like children on a European jaunt in Germany with Liverpool. Barking orders like a prison camp commandant. 'Do ziz, do zat.' The nearest he came to a touch of civility was when he snapped a question at Don 'Iz zis your first visit to Dusseldorf?'

'Actually, no,' said Don. 'But it did look a bit different from a Wellington bomber at 10,000 feet!'

Twenty Two

ANY OTHER BUSINESS

NOT for me, at any rate. I can't imagine I would have made much of a fist of doing anything else and I shall keep 'punching' right to the last bell. Then I might just look for a rematch.

Sport traverses so many frontiers and my only regret is that the newspaper industry seems to be contracting so alarmingly that there will be fewer and fewer opportunities for school leavers who want to follow the same yellow brick road. And the technology is changing so fast. The 'NET' used to be for sticking a ball in, nothing else.

Maybe, if the ambition is strong enough, doors will open but you've got to be prepared to hammer on them first, even kick a few down. Attitude is the thing. As Bruce Rioch told me, when he went into football management after a successful career as a player 'I don't read my stars, I reach for them.' And I liked Barry Venison's profundity, when he was becoming disillusioned with life at Roker Park in the mid 80's. 'If you think champagne, you drink champagne. The trouble is, at Sunderland they think water.'

The power of positive thinking was brought home to me when I was a junior reporter back in my weekly newspaper days in Harrogate. I asked a centenarian what it felt like to be 100 years old and she said 'Well, young man, it's better than the alternative.' Nice one, Alice.

When the megalomaniacs, bullies and head-bangers were having their way at the *Sunday Express*—a not uncommon occurrence in newspapers these days—and making life distinctly unpleasant, staff morale was lower than a snake's belly. The departure of one gloriously unpopular editor was marked with the following epitaph 'we were the willing, led by the unknowing, doing the impossible for the ungrateful.' Our rallying cry in the northern office was 'Don't worry, it'll soon be Sunday.' We weren't exactly victims of the slave trade but everything is relative.

So stay sharp, like the *News of the World* photographer who found himself in a perilous situation up a tree! He had been ordered by his office to stake out a house believed to be the home of a husband and wife who were operating a paedophile ring. His brief was to get a picture of them together.

He shinned up a tree overlooking the house and waited for hours until the wife suddenly appeared in the garden and started watering some plants. The 'snapper' pointed his camera just as an angry voice shouted 'Heh, you. What are you doing taking pictures of my wife?' He looked down and saw the husband, at the foot of the tree, wielding a pick-axe handle.

The photographer's mind worked quicker than his camera shutter. He climbed down without a hint of panic and explained 'No, I'm not taking pictures of your wife, guvnor. We're investigating the couple who live in the house next to yours and I can get a good angle on their garden by looking across yours from this tree.'

By now the irate husband had been joined by his wife, demanding to know what the fuss was about. 'Well, piss off then and take your pictures from somewhere else!' 'Right, sorry,' blurted the 'snapper' from the 'screws'. But here they were, the husband and wife, the suspected paedophiles, right in front of him, together. He couldn't afford to let the opportunity slip.

As the couple walked back into their garden they heard the click of the camera, spun round and saw it pointing straight at them. 'You bastard, I knew you were taking pictures of my missus,' said the husband, wielding the pick-axe again. 'No mate, honest. It's just that this is a new camera and it keeps sticking. Just tell me if you can see the shutter move when I go like this.

CLICK! Oh, it's alright now ... see yer.' The cheek of it.

I admire the 'snappers', more so the sports photographers who only get one split second to capture a goal being scored or a wicket falling, for all their fancy cameras. They sit on their little canvas stools in the pissing rain while scribes like me stay high and dry in the stands. And if they miss the big picture, they're in trouble. No one to help them out, unless they find an unexpected ally in a referee!

A *Daily Express* 'snapper' was so bored with the drudgery of a game at Port Vale a few years ago that he fell asleep on his stool beside one of the goals. The next thing he felt was a tap on the shoulder. It was the referee. 'Wake up, pal, I've just awarded a penalty and since you're the only photographer here, I thought you would want a picture of it.'

It must be a great feeling to capture the goal of the season or the sports picture of the year. Me? I'll stick to holiday snaps and the written word. I like the cryptic humour of the press box when a game is less than edifying. I was at a night match at Halifax and after nearly an hour of excruciating boredom and rank bad football, there was a little flurry of action close to the touchline, three or four passes, a good cross and a header just over the bar. The old Yorkshire scribe sitting next to me, who had suffered this level of football for 40-odd years, took a long, slow puff on his pipe and offered the opinion 'Do you know ... for a few moments there I think they actually knew what they were trying to do!'

That lovely cynicism was matched by Les Barlow of the *Rochdale Observer* when I was covering a cup tie at Spotland and the Dale scored an extraordinarily good goal. Just to make sure I had identified the right player in the build-up, I asked Les: 'Who played that great pass across the box to Painter?' Les answered, deadpan: 'Pass? I don't think it was a pass. The ball just ricocheted off his shins.'

Ron Kennedy, another fine northern journalist, who has covered the chequered careers of Burnley and Blackburn for decades has always written from the heart, and he did a superb intro for the *Sunday Express* on a game so abysmal I cannot recall the teams or the score. But I can remember the intro. It read: 'There are times when a man needs the hand of restraint upon his shoulder before committing his thoughts to paper.'

The mention of Blackburn revives memories of Ewood Park before Jack Walker's millions transformed a crumbling eyesore into a fine, new stadium and provided a team to match. It was almost a throwback to the days of clogs and shawls when cotton was king. Even when Kenny Dalglish was installed as manager, in 1991, the manager's and secretary's offices were in a terraced house, No 110 Nuttall Street. And, for a while, the manager's after-match press conference was conducted similarly, in a lounge on the ground floor.

Keith Meadows, then a 'staffer' with the *Daily Mirror* in Manchester will never be allowed to live down the tale that he wandered in half an hour after a game, helped himself to a beer from the sideboard and started making idle chat with a man sitting in an armchair watching television. 'Funny,' said Keith. 'I thought the other lads would be here by now.' 'What other lads and who the f****** hell are you?' asked the man in the armchair of our cloth-capped hero. Keith had only gone into the wrong house, hadn't he?

Some pressmen have a delightfully sardonic streak as demonstrated by Keith Donnolly of the *Daily Express* just after Mick Mills had become the new manager of Stoke City in 1985. Under the previous regime it had been difficult for the press to get access to the players for after-match quotes. The likeable Mills wanted to redress the situation. So after a fairly parlous opening game the disenchanted press were asked if there were any particular Stoke players they would like to see. Keith, quick as a flash, replied 'Yes, Neil Franklin and Stanley Matthews.'

The razor-sharp Bob Cass—a final plug for the *Mail on Sunday*—loves a bit of verbal sparring and usually has the last laugh. Newcastle United were so thrilled when Kevin Keegan joined them as a player in the mid-80's, one of their officials opened the press conference with the ditty 'We're in heaven because we've signed Kevin,' to which Bob countered 'It's a good job you haven't signed Richie Pitt!'

Sharp minds are the source of many one-liners, published or otherwise, and a special prize goes to the Fleet Street icon who proved that even a stab of pain could not dull his creative talent. Arriving at London's Cafe Royale restaurant, for the Footballer of the Year Dinner, he was confronted in the foyer by a bitter rival, who aimed a kick at his groin. As the recipient of the kick went down, doubled up in agony, he was heard to gasp 'You are a bastard xxxx, but I admire your choreography!'

There is not too much to be admired about the press these days but I still maintain that newspapers, whether you buy them to be informed or entertained or regard them as comics, are cheap at the price. Think about that the next time you buy a pint, a packet of fags or even a cup of tea.

And good writers, good writing, good pictures and good editing deserve a better fate than to wrap up a portion of fish and chips. It is every bit as much of a talent to write quickly, informatively, stylishly and accurately under pressure as it is to perform.

Hunter S. Thompson does not come into that category. He wrote 'With a few rare exceptions, sports writers are a kind of rude, brainless sub-culture of fascist drunks.' I am among those consulting their lawyers. No one calls me 'rude' and gets away with it.

Postscript:

It's been great fun sharing a few tales with you about sport and sports writing. And as that lovely Irish comedian Jimmy Cricket would say: 'Come here ... there's more!'